People not cases

Welfare and Philosophy
The International Library of

General Editors

Professor Noel Timms
Professor of Social Work,
University of Newcastle upon Tyne

David Watson
Department of Moral Philosophy,
University of Glasgow

People not cases
a philosophical approach
to social work

Nicholas M. Ragg

Senior Lecturer in Applied Social Studies
University of Surrey

Routledge & Kegan Paul
London, Henley and Boston

First published in 1977
by Routledge & Kegan Paul Ltd
39 Store Street,
London WC1E 7DD,
Broadway House, Newtown Road,
Henley-on-Thames,
Oxon RG9 1EN and
9 Park Street,
Boston, Mass. 02108, USA
Printed in Great Britain
by Redwood Burn Limited
Trowbridge & Esher

ISBN 0 7100 8482 X

Contents

Preface

This book runs the risk of being mistaken for what it is
not intended to be. It is not a textbook on social work
although the final chapters attempt to delineate a broad
approach to the discipline. It is not simply a philosophical analysis of social casework because it does set
forth a specific approach: on the basis of an analysis of
social-casework periodicals and a philosophical analysis
an attempt is made to formulate a specifically personal
approach to social work.

The book was written with a readership of philosophers
and social workers in mind. Philosophers will find little
original in it philosophically, but they may be interested
in the attempt to base a practical activity on philosophy.
Social workers will be familiar with much in the passages
descriptive of social work. I hope that the result of
writing for two disciplines is not that what is said is of
interest for neither.

There are many people who have helped in the writing of
this book. David Watson, one of the editors of this
series, gave unstintingly of his time and thought in going
through manuscripts and typescripts. Without his detailed
and pertinent comments, philosophers would be far more
critical than they no doubt will and should be. Alan
Milne spent many hours discussing the original project
with me and listening to early versions. Readers familiar
with his own work will realise my indebtedness to him.
Needless to say I am responsible for all the errors and
inconsistencies in the pages that follow.

Personal experience of working with different people
has also profoundly influenced my ideas. I must include,
in any list of such experiences, working in the Department
of Psychiatry at Manchester University under Professor
E. E. Anderson. Here I was put in touch with the
possibility of developing practical applications of

philosophy. My amateur interest in the discipline
originated there. I must also include the experience of
group work and family therapy, especially some months
spent working in one of the county teams of Dingleton
Hospital, Melrose. Finally, I shall never forget the
experience of working with various members of the Bally-
murphy Tenants' Association in an advice centre. They
brought home to me the extent to which social-work skills
can be self-learned, and they taught me the importance of
seeing social work within a framework of social justice.

What I have attempted to do in this book is to solve a
long-standing dilemma in social work - the social worker's
dual allegiance to the individual client and to society.
I hope I have shown that concern for the first as a person
entails a stance towards the second such that conduct vis-
à-vis society is entailed in enhancing and developing
personal identity.

I have adopted no party political or ideological stance
in this book, though the writing of it, and the
experiences that contributed to the writing of it, have
since led me to adopt such a stance. What I hope the book
shows is that because a personal approach to social work
demands a critical stance towards society a political
position is a likely consequence. Social theory, Marxist
or otherwise, explains why society or large parts of it,
does not offer an environment fit for personal life. It
is the purpose of what follows to attempt to set out the
conditions necessary for personal life to become
established and develop. The task of explaining why such
conditions do not materialise is another story, and one to
which politics may provide the answer.

I have used the term 'client' throughout the book for
want of a better one. It is, in fact, antipathetic to my
theme, which develops the idea that social worker and
client should endeavour to relate to each other as persons
and equals, rather than as professional and client.

At the outset of the book I have used social work and
social casework as different terms. In the latter part
they are used more or less synonymously as my argument is
that treating people as people is a moral and rational
exercise vitiated by technical therapeutic approaches such
as that of social casework.

My thanks are also due to Mrs Glenys Brook for her
patience and speed in producing the typescript and to
Mrs M. E. Franklin for preparing the index.

1 Introduction: the person in social work

'People not cases' has long been a slogan of social caseworkers. Reference to the person or the personal has been
continuous in social-work journals since the end of the
Second World War. In this chapter I have selected some
examples of letters and articles in these journals that
illustrate both the continuity of concern with the topic
and also different notions of how to help people as
people. Many of the references and quotations that follow
arose as the 'new' casework techniques were adopted by
different groups of the profession. While these 'new'
methods had been present in the country since 1929, it was
not until after the Second World War that they really
began to affect practice at field level   (E. Irvine,
'Social Work', July 1956).

   The first examples are taken from early numbers of 'The
Almoner'. Concern that people should be treated as people
emerged out of a general discussion about how the medical
social worker should accommodate to the new institutions
of the welfare state. The question was whether or not she
should give up her 'general welfare functions' and engage
in 'intensive medical social casework', surrendering
administrative duties and joining the medical treatment
team. The editorial of the June 1948 issue relates that
'the Institute of Almoners had clearly laid it down in its
statement on the almoner's function that "she should be
allotted only such administrative duties as relate
directly to her function of helping the doctor in the
treatment of the patient" '. A letter in the August 1948
issue bears the same message: 'we must be recognised as
specialists in the team which seeks to restore the
maximum creative function, and day-to-day hospital
arrangements cannot be our responsibility. By all means
let some other branch of Welfare Worker be appointed....'

   In June 1951 Miss O'Farrel gave a comprehensive account

of Social Casework in a Medical Setting. She wrote:

> The role of the caseworker is to sit down with the
> patient and help him to work out his difficulty in his
> own way, not imposing her will or her goals on him but
> looking at the whole situation from his angle and
> helping him to recognise and remove from his path those
> obstacles personal or material which impede his
> recovery and prevent his full co-operation with the
> doctor.

This is the first full statement in 'The Almoner' by a
British caseworker of the new casework approach. Laymen
might well have wondered what the casework relationship
was if not friendship.

And yet it was this move to 'intensive medical social
casework' that gave rise to a concern for the personal.
Many feared that the new 'scientific' techniques would
interfere with the 'intuitive' personal relationship
between almoner and patient that developed as the almoner
went about her 'general welfare functions' on the
patient's behalf. In response to this accusation of not
treating people as people the new professional caseworkers
developed the idea of treating 'the whole person'. An
illustration of the fear appears in the report of a
conference in the May 1950 issue. Miss Stirling is
reported to have said:

> There seems to me to be a real danger of doing more
> harm than good by dealing pseudo-scientifically with
> matters for which we have not been specially trained
> and if we were so trained there might be a risk that we
> might have a colder and more analytical approach to our
> patients. One of our most useful assets in the past
> has been that we have been just ordinary people like
> themselves and not either doctors or psychologists.

In the June 1950 issue came the response of the new
professionals. Miss Gatliff was a psychiatric social
worker and therefore trained in the new methods. She
wrote:

> It seems to me that we are in danger of forgetting that
> the patient is a whole person and that it is the
> special function of any social worker to see him in
> this way. His many practical needs are well known to
> us.... He may require help in his personal relation-
> ships and family adjustments ... yet the assessment of
> any of these needs can best be made by one trained to
> consider him in his personal and family setting.

In the last quotation the conflict between 'general
welfare functions' and 'intensive medical casework' is
solved by the idea of helping the whole person in his
social setting. The concept of the whole person has still

to be fully developed. It is clear, however, that it
involves helping him both practically and with his
relationships.

In April 1950 two articles appeared in 'Social Work'
which illustrated the tension between the new 'scientific'
and the traditional 'intuitive' approaches to social work.
The first of these is by Robert J. N. Todd, and called Why
Visit? In the text there is evidence of the move away
from a 'practical' approach to a psychological one:

the most important factor in any social problem with
which a client needs help is not so much the actual
size of the problem itself but the client's attitude to
it. The worker's understanding of this will only be
furthered by the client's ability to reveal both his
hopes and his fears about his problem and also his
drive towards his solution. The extent to which he
will be able to do this will depend upon the relationship that is built up between the client and the
worker.

Todd also exemplified how caseworkers working in the new
way talked as if they were dealing not with people but
with attitudes and other generalised psychological
processes and forces:

There is probably more than one way of dealing with
such hostile attitudes. There are those who feel that
such people are the victims of society and require more
understanding and more love from the caseworker. She
may try to convey this by being more outgoing and by
re-assuring the client over points about which she
feels he is in doubt or uncertain.... Such action on
the part of the worker may cause the client to feel
guilty over previously half-experienced hostility and
he will then appear to respond with warmer feelings.

This question illustrates not only how caseworkers were
inclined to treat clients as the vehicles of guilt or
hostility, but also how psychologically orientated the
work could become. Even when Todd alludes to social
aspects of casework it is in terms of general categories:
'At the risk of over-simplification a distinction should
be made between work which is aimed at environmental
adjustment and work which is aimed at the adjustment of
emotional attitudes ....' Todd conveyed the impression of
the caseworker remaining coolly detached from the client,
trying to change attitudes, adjust behaviour, or modify
the environment. This detachment is conveyed by the words
used: adjustment, diagnostic process, worker-client
relationship, etc. There is no description of the client
as an experiencing person.

In sharp contrast, in the same issue Mary Richardson

writes about her work with four families:

The two main factors in each of my four families were
financial hardship, with very poor material standards
in the home and the weariness that comes of living and
rearing a family against that background. The mother
becomes worn out from standing up to constant criticism
and beaten down by the consciousness of failure to
conform to the standards demanded of her.... The sense
of inferiority and failure to conform results in
bitterness against society whose demands and criticisms
have registered the failure and the degree of
inferiority, and a loss of faith in the validity of the
virtues of kindness and honesty. My first aim in each
case has been to relieve the pressure of material
necessity, because there can be no spiritual
rehabilitation in the face of constant physical wearing
down. At the same time ... to induce the ability to
accept thankfully the help offered by society which it
has come to hate and from that to pass on ... to make
its own contribution to society.

Establishing confidence with a woman who has been
subject to criticism and hostility from all sides may
take many months, and I would say to evoke it at all
the client must recognise in the worker a pure desire
to help, not improve, an absence of any axe to grind,
and a complete reliability over practical plans and
details. There has to be a sense of timelessness in
the worker so that she really feels both that there is
no time limit for what she is trying to do, and that
her object is real and important enough to be willing
to progress through the smallest details. It is based
on spiritual values, the value of each person as a
person - and only secondarily as a potential
contributor to the community.... The practical aspect
of it needs some adaptation of normal casework
practice. If you have a delicate mother of a large
family in bad accommodation ... there are some things
which must be done ... the provision of such aids to
washing as a copper and a wringer.... There should be
chairs to enable all the family to sit at the same
time....

These quotations reflect a fairly widespread
professional concern centring round the introduction of
the new casework methods. The contrast between Robert
Todd's and Mary Richardson's papers illustrates the
difference in approach. Once more a concern for the
person can be perceived at the heart of the discussion.
Robert Todd described his clients in terms of certain
psychological forces of which they appeared to be the

vehicles. He treated them by manipulating these forces.
His instrument was the relationship and he suggested
ways of interacting with the client to achieve this
manipulation and the consequent adjustment of the client's
behaviour. He did not attempt to describe the client's
experience. Mary Richardson, on the other hand, described
her mothers in everyday language, not in terms of
psychological forces. She emphasised their experience:
bitterness, failure, sense of inferiority, lack of faith
in kindness and honesty. This experience she saw as
generated by society's rejection of the mothers rather
than by their own internal psychological processes.
Robert Todd described the caseworker as trying to achieve
emotional or environmental adjustment. Mary Richardson
said she was aiming for spiritual rehabilitation. This
seems to have consisted in overcoming the mothers'
bitterness against society and sense of inferiority: 'A
restoration to her of the feeling of having a rightful
place in the world.' It also appears to have involved a
restoration of faith in the validity of the values of
honesty and kindness. This was achieved through the
relationship between caseworker and client, though not by
manipulating psychological forces. Mary Richardson
described how the relationship should give expression to
fundamental values and as a result restore the client's
confidence in the possibility of people being honest,
helpful, and true to their word. The caseworker must have
a pure desire to help, with no personal axe to grind -
that is, to be sincere, honest and straightforward; the
caseworker must be completely reliable over plans and
details - that is, keep his promises of future action and
stick to his word; the caseworker should have a sense of
timelessness (perhaps unending patience) - this came from
valuing the client as a person and not, in the first
instance, as a potential contributor to society. This
meant that the mothers were valued for what they were:
individual people with unique, and in this case tragic,
experience behind them. Helping them consisted in
helping them to achieve a better experience of society for
their own sake, not to make them better mothers or wage-
earners, etc. Initially this better experience came
through the relationship with the caseworker, in which the
above values were realised.
     Alasdair McIntyre (1967, p.95) has described the values
mentioned by Mary Richardson as fundamental in the sense
that without them co-operation between men, and therefore
society itself, would in principle be impossible. He
argues that honesty, promise-keeping and the deprecation
of violence are values without the realisation of which

co-operation between men would be impossible. It is
therefore of inestimable importance in any attempt to
describe how to 'treat people as people' that these basic
values should be given great emphasis. Mary Richardson
was emphasising them, and in doing so she was maintaining
that the casework relationship was a personal one. She
was working with people as the subjects of experience and
the holders of values and beliefs; not as the vehicles of
psychological processes and forces.

Now, it does not necessarily follow that by adopting
Todd's approach Mary Richardson's is ruled out, but it is
easy to think that it is. If the caseworker became solely
concerned to diagnose psychological processes and
conflicts, personality types, etc., the significance of
the client as a person would be denied. It is by
recognising that the client has beliefs, feelings and
thoughts that he is treated as a person - thus the
importance of getting to know what a person thinks, what
the client thinks, in treating any individual as a person;
for only persons have thoughts and beliefs about themselves and the world around them.

Other caseworkers argued that the new approach was
quite compatible with the old. Betty Joseph was, perhaps,
the person most responsible for introducing psychoanalysis
into casework in Britain, through her teaching on the LSE
Mental Health Course evacuated to Cambridge during the
Second World War. She writes ('Social Work', April 1951):

once we really achieve a psychoanalytic theory of human
growth we also achieve a far greater respect for
individuals and for the agonies involved in growing
into a mature human being, and our attitude in casework
shifts from giving advice on behaviour from above to
trying to understand the problems of the client from
where he stands and from what he feels.

In the same issue of 'Social Work' Elizabeth Howarth,
in another important article, takes the same line. The
same criticism, however, may be made. These views are
based on a theoretical construct - a psychoanalytic
explanation of man. Miss Joseph and Miss Howarth were
both using a theory about what makes human beings work, to
understand the client and his situation. The result of
the theory may have been that more respect was paid to the
individual not in terms of his experience but in terms of
psychological processes and forces, especially ones of
which he was unconscious. With this specialist knowledge
and theory, the caseworker aspired 'to see behind to what
kind of people they are'. The theory left the caseworker
'outside' the client's situation. He was the detached,
specialist observer. He was not involved in the approach

of one human being to another; he was not an ordinary
person like the clients to whom he talked. Yet it was
this characteristic of being ordinary that was said by
traditional caseworkers to be their greatest asset.

In April 1962 there appeared in 'Social Work' the first
attempt to deal at length with what may be involved in
attempting to offer 'personal' help to someone else. It
was in an article by Margaret Tilley entitled Religion and
the Social Worker:

> There is of course one value about which all social
> workers, whether Christian or not, are in fundamental
> agreement; the value of a person for himself alone,
> not for his worth to the community, not for his use as
> an object, not as a means to an end, but simply because
> he is alive.... How easy is it to value people for
> themselves? Can this kind of claim easily deteriorate
> into a cliché? Certainly the more experience one has
> in social work the more one realises the dangers of
> this. It is often taken more or less for granted that
> an averagely kind person wants to help those in trouble,
> and casework teaching concentrates on methods and
> skills for doing this effectively and appropriately.
> But is our basic attitude necessarily so benevolent?
> It is anyhow practically impossible to see another
> person as fully real as oneself and not just as the
> object of one's passing attention and this may be
> particularly true when dealing with people whose
> humanity has been diminished by their misfortunes. The
> danger of wrong involvement in the casework situation
> is often stressed but much less said about what happens
> when the right kind of involvement is absent. Julia de
> Beausobre makes a distinction between the English and
> Russian way of expressing pity for suffering: 'Pity is
> indeed one of the outstanding virtues of the English;
> but it is not, and must not be personal; to be good it
> must be social and the giver must not lose caste in the
> giving.' On the other hand the Russian who feels pity
> 'must leave his own place among the good people on the
> sunny side of the gap and must go out and find the
> other where he is - in the darkness on the side of evil
> - and be ready to stay with him there'. Julia de
> Beausobre goes on to explain that participation of this
> kind acts as a redemptive force in the world. It is an
> interesting theme but one that at first glance appears
> remote from modern social casework with its emphasis on
> diagnosis or assessment of need in the individual and
> on methods for meeting this. The right assessment of
> need, however, depends on having the right kind of
> knowledge and a great deal goes into acquiring this

knowledge which can never be just an intellectual exercise. One has to enter imaginatively into another person's experience and this requires a particular form of involvement which has its own hazards. There are many reasons for wishing to avoid involvement with others; time, energy and money can be spent elsewhere with more profit to oneself; status and reputation may be damaged; more subtly there is the impact on deep feelings both known and unsuspected producing anxiety or hostility. Some situations and conditions easily elicit sympathy but there are others which arouse fear, repulsion and shock.... Although a social worker is equipped by her training to understand ... yet she may well have to wrestle with her natural reactions and will continually have to watch a tendency to over-build her defences....

This was an important contribution to the discussion. and not only because it was a direct attempt to understand what may be involved in helping another as a person. Something like the distinction made by the traditional caseworkers between helping as an 'ordinary person' and being a 'scientific' helper was made again here. The new 'scientific' caseworker assessed need from a detached position, whereas 'personal' help, ideally, involved joining the other person oneself, as a person, 'in the darkness'. At least it required imaginatively entering his experience. Nor are the difficulties encountered in attempting this sort of help technical ones. They affect the caseworker personally: his time and resources, his status, his feelings and personal experience. Helping personally, as described by Margaret Tilley, seemed to be helping by being an ordinary person like the client and not becoming another specialist.

In April 1963 Ruth Wilkes introduced into the debate some ideas that derive from existentialism. She also deplored the use of terms such as 'social science', 'social statistics' and argued that it was on the use of such terms that a caseworker's claim to be a specialist was based. She claimed that the personal in each human being could not be rendered by scientific analysis and inquiry and that if the caseworker stopped doing what he did in order to analyse and objectify it, he would cease to be able to do it. She explains:

Society always desires to be totalitarian. No-one has understood this better than that lone swimmer, Søren Kierkegaard: 'This is what it (the age) aspires to: it would build up the established order, abolish God, and through fear of men cow the individual into a mouse's hole.' I know of no argument to convince an

unbeliever that there is an element in the individual
which is capable of rising above the collective. By
whatever way - religious, philosophical or political -
you arrive at this conclusion, in the end it is something you see or do not see. The existence or non-
existence of this element within the individual is not
the kind of truth that can be made the object of
inquiry to be proved or disproved beyond all doubt, and
for that reason its consideration is not acceptable in
a scientific age.

Writers such as Elizabeth Howarth and Betty Joseph
argued that the new methods enhanced the professional's
respect for the client as a person. While their method
was attacked for not taking into account social and interpersonal factors, people like Margaret Tilley and Ruth
Wilkes mounted a more radical objection: the personal
element in human beings cannot be rendered by science, and
since casework is concerned with persons, science is
irrelevant. Though this was probably a new beginning
deriving from existential philosophy it obviously
resonates in sympathy with the 'intuitive' approach of the
traditional caseworkers. These themes were argued in
greater detail in the 'British Journal of Psychiatric
Social Work'.

In two articles ('BJPSW', vol.I, no.1, 1947 and vol.I,
no.3, 1949) in very early numbers, Miss F. E. Waldron
appears to refer to the old intuitive tradition of social
work, but puts it in the newer context by suggesting that
an ordinary human relationship can indeed be used in
helping:

The patient, our material, is made of the same human
stuff as ourselves, and must be responsive or unres-
ponsive according to the particular way he is acted
upon by his fellow human beings. We have no tools
except our own personalities to bring about this
responsiveness, and our detachment referred to above as
the primary character controlling our draughtsmanship,
has to be modified by the necessity to use our personalities in forming a relationship with our material.

In her second article, Miss Waldron described the importance of not becoming 'blind and deaf to the sights and
sounds of our daily life', 'that is the common experience
of her patient's social group, neighbourhood group, and
racial or religious group'. She seems to be pleading that
in developing therapeutic techniques and in sociological
understanding of the patient's predicament, life as it is
lived should not be ignored. A therapeutic relationship
is also a human one; a sociological description does not
render life as it is lived.

In another article ('BJPSW', vol.II, no.9, 1953) Mrs
Lederman further explored how the patient could be helped
as a person through a personal relationship, rather than a
detached therapeutic one. Throughout the discussion she
maintained that in order to make the relationship with the
client personal, the caseworker had to be prepared to
express his own feelings, positive and negative. This
particular development culminated in an article in 'BJPSW'
(vol.V, no.1, 1959) entitled Relationship Therapy and
Casework. Using the notion of role, T. A. Ratcliffe
developed the idea of being a 'real professional person'
with a parental role providing a model of the worker-
client relationship. 'Advice-giving, approval, reproof
and reassurance must all be considered in relationship to
the client's needs' within the general parental-type
relationship. The parental role was chosen as a model
because it was one in which the client (like the child)
might grow, learning lessons that he had not learned, or
had mislearned, in his own childhood.

'Role' is a new idea in the discussion: the caseworker
fulfils the role of a professional person. From this it
can be inferred that there is something of him outside the
role - that the role of professional person does not
involve him fully as a person. Ratcliffe also makes it
clear that what the caseworker does in fulfilling his role
in relationship therapy is decided by technical criteria
derived from his specialist knowledge of child-rearing and
interpersonal interaction. The aim appears to be to
influence the client's psychological make-up by providing
a corrective social environment - the therapeutic
relationship. This is quite different from the moral or
ethical objectives of the relationship between client and
worker described by Mary Richardson. Her purpose was to
give expression to certain fundamental human values.

Miss Goldberg ('BJPSW', vol.III, no.1, 1955) describes
American experience in a way which can be seen as an
attempt by the scientific approach to treat the client as
a 'whole person'. She writes:

In the States great efforts are made in psychiatry, the
social and biological sciences, to see the human being
once more as a complete organism in his total setting.
I found that psychiatry had entered a new and exciting
phase of ever closer co-operation and integration with
the biological sciences on the one hand and the social
sciences on the other.

We psychiatric social workers became deeply absorbed
in the use of our therapeutic relationship with the
individual client.... Have we paid sufficient
attention to the interaction of the whole family, or

the cultural traditions and pressures surrounding our
clients, or the importance of extra-familial figures,
such as the peer group in late adolescence?
Miss Goldberg then went on to show how, both in research
and practice in the USA, an attempt was being made to
perceive the client by way of all the social science
disciplines, and psychodynamically. This, however, was a
different issue from that of relating to the client as a
person and helping him personally; it was an attempt to
see the client 'as a complete organism in his total
setting'.

In the 'British Journal of Psychiatric Social Work' two
different solutions to the problem of treating the client
as a person were proposed. Relationship therapy was the
fruit of an attempt to get away from the detachment of
therapist and patient that was thought to exist in
psychoanalysis. It put the caseworker in the position of
himself being an instrument of therapy rather than being
the wielder of these instruments. It was but a variation
on the 'scientific' approach so much feared by the
traditional workers, albeit a more human variation. Miss
Goldberg's exposition of treating the whole person appears
to have rather different origins. It was an attempt to
overcome the dichotomy between the individual and his
social environment. The therapists' idea of treating the
whole person seems to have grown out of the debate between
the supporters of a practical, welfare-based social work
and the promoters of 'intensive casework' with its
emphasis on treating the client's individual psycho-
pathology. Treating the client as a whole person in Miss
Goldberg's sense involved considering him as the product
of his social and physical environment; it also involved
interpreting him in this environment through a battery of
specialist disciplines. Neither of these approaches fully
meets the criticisms of the traditional workers, for
neither emphasises the moral values on which personal
existence depends and the realisation of which was the aim
of Mary Richardson's social casework.

Ruth Wilkes ('Social Work Today', vol.1, no.8, November
1970) argued that one of the problems the caseworker had
to deal with was the sense of isolation that afflicts
many people. This she saw as part of a great historical
development in which man, from the corporate experience
of medieval times, emerged at the Renaissance as an
individual. He experienced himself and treated others
as individual persons, not as the representatives of a
feudal class or a guild. With this experience of
individuality came the sense of isolation; 'and it is
thought that "group feeling" or "community spirit" is

somehow a good way of dealing with this problem'. She
goes on to ask: 'What is the philosophy behind these
ideas and how does it relate to the acceptance of the
individual as a unique being to be treated as an end in
himself? In other words we are faced with the problem of
finding ways in which unique and separated individuals can
relate to each other without losing their separate
identities.' In trying to solve this problem she rejected
traditional philosophy, the 'scientific' approach and
ethical theory. Instead she turned to existentialist
philosophy for an answer: 'The existential triad of the
unique, the other and communication between them.' Miss
Wilkes appears to have seen a danger of the ultimate value
of the individual being lost in the new 'group' and
'community' methods. In their place she puts the meeting
of two persons and what happens to them as persons. She
eschews the attempt of one person to do something to
another:

> The kind of healing Buber has in mind takes place
> through the meeting of one person with another rather
> than through insight and analysis. The situation is
> transformed when something in the other person comes
> alive in me. This view of Buber's is capable of much
> development which could be of value to social work. It
> is clearly not the way of the expert whose theoretical
> knowledge puts him in a superior position to the person
> he is trying to help. Equally, it is not the way of
> one who seeks to intervene in the life of another,
> either by helping him to some kind of 'adjustment' or
> by changing his environment. It is an important view
> in connection with group work and community work
> because it makes the philosophical background of human
> dignity the same for individual casework and for work
> with people in groups.

This paper is important for the theme we are trying to
follow for it states quite clearly that it is what goes
on between caseworker and client as persons that is
important in casework and not any expertise in human
relations. It is interesting too that Ruth Wilkes related
this approach not only to casework but also to group and
community work. The importance of the personal approach
she emphasised later: 'Personal relations between
individuals assume equality between them and there can be
no question of one interpreting the other by means of this
or that theory.'

> It follows that if we are to understand each other we
> can only try to know our own thoughts and feelings with
> all possible honesty so that we are able to convey them
> to others by our words and behaviour. We understand

each other not by the theorising of the detached
observer but through inter-subjectivity.
She argued that: 'The link between unique and solitary
individuals is not a sense of identity but a sense of
responsibility.... But there can be no responsibility as
long as deterministic modes of thought prevail and man
remains imprisoned in the world of causality....' Finally
she maintained that 'the problem of social work is not how
to find ways in which personality can be developed in
society; the problem is to consider how unique and
separated individuals can act responsibly towards each
other'. Responsibility she saw as being exercised by
careful criticism of another person's beliefs. To
criticise a person, however carefully, for his beliefs, is
to ask him to change himself. She could see no valid
distinction between a person's belief and the theory he
held, for a theory was 'so much part of an individual's
belief and approach to life that it cannot be something
taught in one place and related to experience somewhere
else'. Thus, change in social work came about not through
the application of learned theory but by the careful
criticism by one person of another person's beliefs - or
so it appears from what she writes. However complete a
theory, or number of theories, might be in rendering 'the
whole person', theories inevitably render 'the whole
person' in a way detached from any particular whole
person, and, since casework is with particular people,
caseworker and client must meet as individual people.

Can caseworkers 'treat people as people' and yet base
their practice firmly on a set of theoretical models?
Gilbert Smith ('Social Work Today', vol.2, no.3, 6 May
1971) argued that the latter is essential: 'the social
phenomena with which social work deals have both causes
and consequences and unless these are understood social
work is unlikely to progress far'.

Ruth Wilkes ('Social Work Today', vol.2, no.10, 12
August 1971) wrote:

There may be no entirely satisfactory answer to the
question of how we can have knowledge, as distinct from
experience, of the individual but it is helpful to know
something of the thoughts of those who have had the wit
to recognise that this problem exists. The argument
centres around the methodological differences between
the natural sciences and the human studies and it
cannot be assumed that the methods of the one can be
transferred wholesale to the other. The assumption
that theory in the human studies can first be learned
and then applied to practice in terms of explanatory,
universally valid principles, as though the world were

somehow totally external to oneself, is open to
objection.

This debate she saw as being 'particularly relevant to
social work, which concerns itself with understanding the
individual for his own sake, quite apart from anything
that may condition or explain him'. Ruth Wilkes here
challenged assumptions fundamental to the arguments put
forward by Gilbert Smith and others. By founding social-
casework practice on a cause-and-consequence base he was
equating its methods with those of the physical sciences.
Ruth Wilkes here moved the discussion of what is involved
in 'treating people as people' a stage further. In the
second half of the quotation she refers to what she
thought was the inability of generally applicable ideas to
render the individual situation. She seems to see a
difference in principle between understanding someone for
his own sake, presumably as an individual, and understanding what might explain or have determined him and his
actions. This suggests that a wholly different discipline
of approach may be involved in 'treating people as people'.
As we shall see this is an extremely significant
suggestion.

By way of summary, the debate to which I draw attention
was precipitated by the introduction of the methods of the
new social casework. These were opposed in the first
instance by traditional social workers who reiterated the
importance of practical and material help for the client.
They also argued that where the relationship was concerned
(which was the focus of the new methods) the emphasis on
technique, science and detachment destroyed the ordinary
personal relationship between social worker and client and
an intuitive way of working. The notion of helping 'the
whole person' was developed. Under it the social worker
helped with both practical problems and relationships. In
the hands of Miss Goldberg this approach burgeoned into a
highly sophisticated technical exercise to render the
client and his environment through a multidisciplinary
approach. It was a complete answer to the criticism that
the new methods took no account of social or interpersonal
factors.

It did not, however, answer the criticism that the new
methods destroyed the natural personal relationship
between social caseworker and client. 'Manipulative'
techniques and 'coldly detached' workers came under fire.
The notion of relationship therapy was born, in which the
caseworker offered the client a personal relationship,
albeit a professional one. This was very much an expert
operation and could hardly be said to be very spontaneous
or intuitive, depending on a highly specialised analysis

of what sort of relationship the client needed. It was, however, accepted that what made the relationship personal was that the caseworker contributed his own feelings to the situation, positive or negative.

The most thoroughgoing criticism of the new methods was developed by Ruth Wilkes, supported by Margaret Tilley. It was derived from existentialist philosophy, but evoked the words of the traditional caseworkers when they argued that an ordinary personal relationship would be destroyed by the new methods which used the relationship as an instrument of therapy. It was at first maintained that what is personal is so individual as to be beyond discovery by the generally applicable notions and methods of science. The personal only appears in a relationship between two people. Under attack, Ruth Wilkes then went on to argue that the methods of the human and natural sciences cannot be assumed to be the same. This introduces a philosophical approach to the person.

2

A theory of action and the person

It has to be admitted that man and society can appropriately be studied by the methods of the natural sciences. On the other hand, an increasing number of people are beginning to support the conclusions reached by Ruth Wilkes - though not always drawing them from her premise. The problem is whether a scientific, causal explanation of human behaviour can ever hope to give a complete picture of human activity. Winch (1958) and Melden (1961) are amongst those who have argued that it cannot, because man's conduct acquires character and significance socially. It has, I think, been convincingly argued that human action cannot be reduced to mere bodily movement (e.g. Melden, 1961, pp.56ff.) nor adequately explained in terms of acts of will or volition causing behaviour (e.g. Melden, 1961; Peters, 1958), nor in purely behavioural terms (e.g. Kenny, 1963, pp.101ff.). What will be attempted in this chapter is the establish-ment of the social and moral conditions necessary for personal life to be established and develop.

Philosophers such as Winch (1958) and Melden (1961) have attempted to explain the nature of action by means of the concept of rule-following. Briefly, this approach maintains that a physical movement is an action because of the significance it is given by society. So the driver of a car raising his arm outside his window makes a signal. The movement of the arm is the action that it is because of the social situation in which it is performed. In another social situation the same physical movement might be another action - perhaps that of a guide pointing out an object of interest to tourists. This example shows that meaning is given socially; it also entails that there must be a mutual acceptance as to what is the social situation in which the movement takes place. If there is no common understanding as to what the situation is, the

physical movement may be seen as a different action by
people involved or as no action at all (for not all
physical movements are actions, e.g. tics and nervous
reactions).

Agreement by all concerned as to the nature of a social
situation demands the shared perceptions, values and
meanings of a common culture (Wittgenstein, 1968, sec.241;
Cavell, 1971). Peter Winch (1958, p.29) examines the
impasse of incomprehensibility in which people find themselves when they perceive situations in contradictory ways.

If the character of an action is defined socially it is
also true that it can only occur if an individual performs
it. Signalling takes place because individual motorists
wish to turn corners - and make the correct rule-following
movements (actions). So, though society may define how
something shall be done, individuals do it.

For an individual to follow a rule he must be able to
recognise something as the same as something else. He
must have a consciousness persisting over time capable of
classifying objects, events and actions as the same as
each other in one way or another. He must also have the
intention to do something that others will recognise as
the same as something else in their characterisation of
it.

How do I, as a member of society, know that I am
following the rule or performing the action correctly?
By what others do in response to my attempt, to e.g.
signal. I can only know that I am actually following the
rule, rather than just thinking that I am, through the
response of others. If following cars move over to pass
me on the left I have reason to believe that I have
succeeded in signalling. I do not show my knowledge of
the rule to the driving examiner by explaining it, but by
doing it. To recite the rules of a game is not to prove
that one can play it. In the less formal activities of
everyday life people are minute by minute confirming (and
correcting) each other's performance of everyday
activities.

Rule-following involves learning, not only to do the
same thing but also what counts as the same thing.
Vendler (1967) compares chess with loosely structured
games like Cowboys and Indians. The rules of chess, even
the combinations of moves, are very formal. What counts
as a move in a chess game is always the same. What counts
as playing Cowboys and Indians, however, can very
enormously over time. There is, therefore, a very wide
gap between what was originally learned and doing what
counts as the same thing. Players have constantly to
assess what they are now doing against what they have

done, and have seen done, in the past, and against the current perceptions of others as to what counts as playing the game and what does not. Vendler suggests that this can be done if each player can positively answer the question, 'Am I doing what I would permit others to do?', of any action he performs in the game. In games like Cowboys and Indians, maintaining the consensus about what counts as the game, and whether any particular action will be characterised as a move in the game or not, is very much more difficult than in chess.

The relationship between a particular action and the whole game in Cowboys and Indians is echoed in ordinary life. That I successfully do what I try to do in ordinary life depends, among other things, on my 'reading' the social situation aright - that means being aware of all the changes in perception of society and involved others, in relation to it. For instance, what I can do now, and still be seen to be teaching (by some !) is very different from what it was ten years ago. The relation between action and situation is thus very complex, but the character of the first depends on people sharing under-standing of the second - classifying situations in roughly the same way. If what I do is to be seen as teaching rather than, for example, playing, I must be aware of how notions of what constitutes a teaching situation have changed, and plan my actions accordingly.

These paragraphs emphasise the fundamental importance of mutual agreement (usually tacit and assumed) in the characterisation of social situations, and consequently of actions. This agreement, usually assumed and unrecognised (sometimes experienced as imposed when I succeed in doing not what I am trying to do but what others see me as doing), underlies all social life.

A second point I wish to make relates to the creativity of rule-following activity. Writers such as Szasz (1962) have argued that human life is separated from that of animals by the ability to follow rules. It is not simply the capacity to follow rules that is the distinctive characteristic of human behaviour; it is the capacity to generate new rules and ways of life. This depends on the ability, described above, to do what counts as the same thing. For the first time something is done it cannot be rule-following and, unless someone has the ability to try to do the same thing again, new practices could not develop. Further, when a practice has developed it can proceed through gradual changes as agreement on what counts as the same thing changes.

It is because human action is rule-following with the characteristics described above, that Peter Winch (1958,

ch.3) argues that the methods of the social sciences
differ from the natural sciences. Although no
existentialist, he thereby supports the view pressed by
Ruth Wilkes. He maintains that the subjects of the social
scientist's study have conscious criteria of their own
about what they are doing and by which they classify their
world. A sociologist trying to understand a society has
to find out how the people see their own activities before
he can begin his work. He has to discover what they see
as, for example, prayer or cruelty before he can begin to
study it. Winch differentiates this approach from that of
the natural sciences in which the worker applies his
criteria direct to his subject of study (but see Ryan,
1970, pp.197-8). The oceanographer classifies the movements of the sea as, for example, tidal flow; he does not
have to ask the ocean what it thinks it is doing.

LANGUAGE AND RULE-FOLLOWING

Rule-following behaviour can take place at a non-verbal
level and obviously does. Both animals and human beings
develop complex modes of interaction based on the transmission and recognition of subtle and less subtle signs.
    The development of symbols, that is signs with a
complex cultural meaning (Szasz, 1962, pp.111-12), is a
specifically human achievement and reaches its height in
language. The notions a society or person has of the
world, even the notions of 'world', 'society' and
'person', are possible only because human beings have a
language in which to frame them.
    Linguists, especially followers of Chomsky (1968,
1972), see their task as to account for the nature of
language as a physical 'corpus' in the world. To this end
Chomsky has devised a complex system of grammatical rules
- transformational grammar - to describe 'all and only the
correct sentences of a language'. Chomsky maintains that
once a person has a mastery of language he has at his
command an instrument of free thought in that, unlike
animal communication systems, human language is not
stimulus bound. Language is related to the environment by
the complex relations of appropriateness. The rules of
grammar allow a person to develop an infinite number of
sentences each with its own meaning and meaning potential
(in relation to the environment). Just as learning to
count enables a person to count to numbers he has never
before attained so the rules of language allow the speaker
to utter sentences he has never before heard or uttered.
    Rule-following where language is concerned is complex.

A speaker needs simple confirmation that he is speaking correctly. He also needs a complex confirmation that the meaning of what he has said is, if not appropriate, at least relevant to the situation he is in. So in language and language-based action, the process of confirmation (or correction) takes place on these two levels.

What can be culled from this is that speech is a highly complex form of rule-following behaviour. It requires, in the first instance, mastery of the instrument of language. To achieve this mastery, the individual is dependent on a speech community. This community activates the linguistic ability innate in the human brain. When he speaks, however, accepting the fact that he speaks correctly, a person participates in the rule-following practices described above. For when he speaks a person must logically utter sentences with meanings. What is socially determined is whether these sentences with their meanings are appropriate or relevant to the situation concerned. What a person says may be quite correct and have a clear meaning but be totally inappropriate to the situation. Scmeone who says, 'I don't like it', while eating a rum baba with relish is in this position (until he clarifies the situation by indicating that it is something else that he doesn't like - perhaps the behaviour of the other diners). In a way, where speech is concerned, the freedom of a group of individuals to develop new rule-following practices - do what counts as the same thing in what counts as the same situation - is circumscribed by the necessity to speak correctly, to use the instrument of language properly (though even the rules of language may slowly change as 'common usage' changes).

The linguist, as has been shown, is interested in devising an explanation of 'all and only' the correct sentences of language. They, or at least those of Chomsky's school, leave untouched the relation of this language to the world. Doctors, physiologists, psychologists, sociologists can all have a part in explaining why a particular individual's or group's performance may be imperfect. The philosopher is also interested in the relation of language to the world, but from a different and more general point of view; more general because what he has to say is not about individual performance but about the general significance of language in human life. One view of this is that rejected by Winch (1958); the so-called 'under-labourer' conception of the philosophy of language. Briefly, this states that the natural and social sciences make discoveries about the world or reality which they describe in technical terms. Confusions may arise in the use of these terms and between

different sets of terms. On the under-labourer view of
philosophy it is the philosopher's task to sort out these
confusions. Winch suggests a much more important position
for philosophy. He maintains that when the scientist
makes discoveries about reality, he is making assumptions
about what reality is. There is a front-line conceptual
task to be done in analysing what is meant by 'reality' in
its multifarious uses and what scientists in different
disciplines mean when they say that the results of their
experiments are 'real' or that they have made discoveries
about the 'world'. It is Winch's view of the role of
philosophy that is adopted here.

Winch writes (1958): 'Our idea of what belongs to the
world of reality is given for us in the language we use.
The concepts we have settle for us the form of experience
we have of the world.' Other philosophers (Cavell, 1958;
Anscombe, 1963 ; Vendler, 1967) have also argued that it
is impossible to become acquainted with the world or
reality other than through language. It is impossible to
become acquainted with the 'brute facts' untainted by
language. There is no way of learning them other than
through language. So when the philosopher analyses
concepts used in describing the world, he is in fact
analysing what counts as the world, because there is no
other way in which the world can 'count' for us. As we
cannot comprehend the world except through the concepts we
have of it, conceptual analysis will tell us something
about what must, logically, count as the world for us.
Philosophy can reveal as much about the world as any of
the natural sciences. Such a stance reduces, even
eliminates, the difference between the world and language.

Wittgenstein (1968, sec.18) described the vocabularies
of the natural sciences - chemistry, physics, etc. - as
extensions of language that reveal more of the world to
us. Because philosophy examines the language we already
have, it seems to tell us what we already know because it
is so familiar. Natural science on the other hand extends
what counts as the world as it extends language.

Hampshire (1958, p.24) maintains that language is used
differently when it is used technically. The terms of
specialist disciplines strive for general relevance so
that their relation to the world will be the same whoever
uses them, whenever they are used and wherever they are
used. In psychiatric use the term 'depressed' or
'depression' is given a highly specific relation to the
world. A person is depressed if he has the symptoms of
depression, e.g. early morning waking, diurnal variation,
psycho-motor retardation, etc. The term 'depression' can
only be used psychiatrically when some or all of these

features are deemed present. This example brings out a
number of things about the technical use of language. The
first is that its reference to the world is general,
determined and limited. Specialists of a discipline agree
that a term shall be used in just this way. This use is
included in textbooks and has to be adhered to. Second,
technical terms do not describe or express individual
experience except in so far as it is generally true.
Third, the general, determined, limited (but precise)
definition of technical terms is given in ordinary
language. Technical vocabularies are therefore secondary
to, and dependent on, the ordinary usage in which their
general and specific terms of reference are given.
Ordinary usage is different: in Hampshire's phrase its
reference to the world is indeterminate and infinitely
extendable. Its reference to the world is not determined
as in the technical usage. A dictionary records how a
word is used and how its use has changed. It does not
prescribe how it is to be used. It is not a book of rules.
Of course words such as 'depression' do have a general
usage. 'Depression' is a sortal term – lying between,
say, 'misery' and 'the blues'. In its technical use it
can only be used when the ordained symptoms are deemed to
be present. The circumstances in which it can be used
ordinarily are wide-ranging. They are the circumstances
about which any particular person feels depressed, for, as
Wittgenstein said, emotions have targets (Wittgenstein,
1968, sec.476). They are directed at something or someone. So ordinary usage invites the description of these
circumstances. What supports the use of the word in one
situation may be different from what supports it in
another (as opposed to the generally recognisable features
supporting the technical use). On hearing the
circumstances described, observers may think the word is
being used inappropriately. Ultimately, however, the
speaker must give the last word of explanation of
appropriateness because he has better access to the
circumstances of his life than anyone else.
    So it can be said that there is no clear list of
circumstances about which a person may, ordinarily, say he
feels depressed, equivalent to the definitive list of
symptoms supporting the technical use of the term. What
the speaker must do is convince his audience that the
circumstances he describes are appropriate to the use of
the word 'depressed'. If he cannot do this, then he
cannot convince them that he is depressed. He has to do
more than demonstrate the presence of certain generally
recognisable symptoms; he has to convince people that the
unique combination of circumstances in his life are

sufficient to support the use of the word.   Usually, but
not always, this is obvious.
     In describing his use of the word 'depression', the
speaker is also describing his emotions.   He is saying
what he is depressed about.   What he and his interlocutors
are doing is analysing one of the concepts he has and
discovering what his experience is and characterising it.
So in analysing the concepts a person uses of himself and
the world, he and others make discoveries about him - in
this case the character of his depression.   This
illustrates that while technical usage is the vehicle of a
general understanding, ordinary usage is the vehicle of
our understanding of individuals.   The importance of this
distinction will appear later, with reference to social
casework, when diagnosis and descriptions are contrasted.
     I have attempted to demonstrate that human activity can
only be fully understood in terms of its being rule-
following.   The human activity of speech is based both on
the possession of an innate linguistic capacity and also
on an ability to follow rules.   In speaking, a person
needs two levels of confirmation or correction, the first
as to the linguistic correctness of what he says and the
second as to its appropriateness or relevance to his
social situation.   'Brute facts' are unapproachable except
through language. As the concepts of a language count as
the world a philosophical analysis can make discoveries
about what must, logically, count as the world.   And the
analysis of the concepts held by an individual inform
about his world and himself.   It may well be that he has
false notions about the world.   It is in such cases that
enumeration of the facts and reasonable argument may help
a person.   He may have confused or contradictory beliefs.
Here a philosophical analysis may help.   What must be
insisted on is that where individuals are concerned social
science must begin with a conceptual analysis of their
beliefs.   This informs the inquirer of their world and
social reality.   The social forces and processes producing
this may then be investigated through the conventional
methods of social sciences.
     Strawson (1959) has attempted to deduce characteristics
of the world beyond language through an analysis of its
structure and use.   He argues that the way in which
language relates to the world may reveal things about the
world.   In particular he has attempted to describe the
characteristics of 'the person' by means of this approach.
This offers an alternative approach to this subject at a
time when the logical difficulties of Cartesian dualism
and of behaviourism have seemed insuperable.   Strawson
argues that states of consciousness or experience cannot

form the basis of an understanding of the person. On the
contrary, he holds that the identification of a particular
state of consciousness or experience depends on the prior
identification of a person to own it. The existence of
emotions or sensations as particulars depends on the
existence of a person to own them. We could not talk
about them unless we could also talk about people who
experienced them. They are dependent on a material body
and the language that describes it. Strawson suggests
that the concept of a person is logically primitive in
that persons are a type of persisting material object to
which 'both predicates ascribing states of consciousness
and predicates ascribing corporal characteristics, a
physical situation, etc. are equally applicable to an
individual of that type' (p.102). The concept of a person
is thus prior to that of a state of consciousness and to
that of a material body. Persons are basic particulars in
their own right. A person is not two things - a body and
a state of consciousness - but one thing, an individual
person to whom both physical characteristics and private
experience can be ascribed. It is this logically
primitive basic particular that 'I' refers to.

Strawson (pp.87ff.,104) remarks that a whole range of
attributes is ascribed to persons: actions and intentions;
sensations; thoughts and feelings; perceptions and
memories; location and attitude (or position); also
physical characteristics such as colour, height, weight
and shape. Some of these ascriptions have a broader use
than others: location, attitude and/or position and
physical characteristics can be ascribed to all material
objects.

Such predicates Strawson names M-predicates because
they are used of all material objects, including persons.
M-predicates are 'applied to material bodies to which we
would not dream of applying predicates ascribing states of
consciousness'. All the other predicates which we apply
to persons Strawson calls P-predicates. It is worth
noting that some P-predicates are not solely applied to
persons; they are used of animals also. It is reasonable
to argue that this use in relation to animals is
secondary or derivative as indicated by the term 'anthro-
pomorphism'. This is because animals cannot use the terms
themselves. P-predicates are part of language, and
language, as has been shown, is a rule-following activity.
Animals cannot join in this particular form of rule-
following, so to ascribe states of being to them, which
are classifications of the world and dependent on the
ability to play a certain game (follow certain rules), is
to bring their behaviour (and therefore consciousness of

self and the world) under rules which they cannot in fact
follow. Not being able to follow them they cannot see
themselves or others in the way that this particular game
determines - as having states of consciousness. It is
fair to say that any animal that could speak would be a
person in the sense that it would be able to participate
in the ascription of P-predicates. This digression somewhat anticipates the arguments which follow.

P-predicates can be sub-divided into what I shall call
active P-predicates, which ascribe actions to people ('is
writing', 'is going for a walk', 'is teasing'), and
experiential P-predicates, which ascribe states of
experience ('is angry', 'is in pain', 'is hot', 'is
cheerful', etc.).

Language is a rule-following activity and P-predicates
are part of language. In learning a language a person
learns to ascribe P-predicates to himself and to others.
By doing this he establishes and participates in personal
life. What we call personal life and experience is
brought into existence by the ascription of P-predicates
to others and to oneself, by the performance of the
activities that make these ascriptions true. For instance,
'I am (or he is) going for a walk' is an example of the
ascription of an active P-predicate. Learning to use such
an expression entails knowing what others and oneself must
do to make such an ascription true. So in learning a
language a person learns also the performances that make
uses of it true. We learn to speak and do.

A difficulty with all P-predicates is that they are
ascribed differently in the first person and in the
third. In the third-person use we ascribe them to people
on the basis of what we observe of their behaviour. If I
say 'He is writing', I am referring to certain observable
actions the other person is performing. I know what he is
doing by observation. If I say 'I am writing' I know that
what I say is true but not on grounds of observation. I
do not observe my movements and then say, as a result of
this observation, that I am writing. I know what I am
doing on grounds other than observation.

This point needs some qualification. There are some
P-predicates that we do on occasion ascribe to ourselves
on the basis of observation. When we assess our
characters saying that we are kind or bad tempered,
efficient or careless, we do so on the grounds of self-
observation. Second, having used a P-predicate in the
first person on grounds other than observation, we may
correct it as a result of observing ourselves. If I am
asked what I am doing and say that I am going for a walk
I may quickly correct myself and say, looking at the

envelope in my hand, 'Well, actually, I am going to post this letter.'

ACTIVE P-PREDICATES

How do I know what I am doing when I ascribe an active P-predicate to myself?   I do not perceive my hand making certain movements and say that I am writing.   I do not receive certain sensations through my body and know by them that I am writing, for the sensations may be the same even though I am performing very different actions; e.g. in writing and in drawing, and in raising my arm to signal and in raising it to point to someone.   The sensations may also be the same as between an action and a random contact with the world, e.g. in being stung while picking a nettle and being stung by a chance contact with it.   When I say, 'I am writing' I am grasping a rule in practice or, rather, two rules.   I am grasping linguistic practice by uttering the sentence correctly.   I am also grasping the rule-following performance of writing by doing it.   This is because active verbs are ascribed to actions, not happenings or natural objects.   It is what I am doing that makes the sentence true.   In order to understand this it is necessary to examine the learning of language.   Melden (1961, ch.13) points out that we do not learn active verbs from the dictionary; we learn them in practice.   We learn what writing means by seeing other people do it and then by doing it ourselves.   We learn both the other-ascription of the verb and the self-ascription.   We learn what the other person must be doing for us to use the verb of him.   However, in learning the self-ascription of the verb (the first-person use) - we have to learn to perform the necessary actions ourselves.   We cannot say, 'I am writing' with truth until we have in fact learned to do so.   The same is true of interpersonal activities like 'teasing'.   I learn the meaning of this verb by having it done to me and seeing others being teased.   I then go away and practise the self-ascription.   Again I learn what I have to do in order to make the use of the word appropriate.   But with interpersonal verbs like this I have also to learn that what may be 'teasing' my little sister is 'insulting' my grandmother.   The concept does not specify any exact performance.   Just as we have to carry the use of words from familiar to unfamiliar situations so we have to carry the performances that active verbs specify.   Active verbs are like a mould into which our unformulated behaviour is poured.   We perform the concepts; the concepts formulate our behaviour.

Active P-predicates create the actions to which they refer when used. In doing this there is a double necessity for the presence of others. It is the other person who not only confirms that we are using the words according to the rules of language but also confirms (or corrects) that we are performing correctly, in the situation, the actions to which the predicate refers. Very often the confirming or correcting response comes in the complementary action of others. If I am trying to tease my sister and she laughs uproariously at me, it slowly dawns on me that I am not 'teasing' her but I am possibly seen as 'joking'. On the other hand, her laughter might be of a sort to be taken as a counter-measure in which case I do receive confirmation that I am teasing. Confirmation would also be received if she cried, or ran away.

Confirmation of the one action is given by the performance of another. One rule-following performance can only be confirmed as rule-following by another rule-following performance. In responding to each other with P-predicates we confirm each other as people. In order to be a person myself, I need the presence of others to confirm the active P-predicates that I perform. In provoking this response in others I invoke them as persons - beings capable of the performance of P-predicates. Active P-predicates are thus at the centre of our treat-ment of each other as people.

In the other ascription of active P-predicates, we proceed on grounds of observation. I have to follow the practices of language correctly, but I do not myself have to put on a performance to make the description true. I need also the confirmation of others that I am using the language correctly. It may be, however, that I am bringing someone's performance under a rule that he is not in fact following. Further observation and perhaps a question or two would ascertain this. Once more it is necessary for us both to be rule-following creatures for this sort of confirmation to take place.

Being able to understand speech is a pre-requisite for both parties, of either the self- or other-ascription of P-predicates. What I ascribe to others on grounds of observation, they grasp in action. I can only truly ascribe active P-predicates to beings capable of doing this and they can only be ascribed to me by others while I remain capable of performing what is ascribed to me. Thus, as Strawson says, neither the self, nor the other ascription of P-predicates, comes first. We have to be able to use them in both first- and third-person practice if we are to use them at all.

In learning a language I learn the self- and other-ascription of active P-predicates. And in order to use them properly I must be able to perform the activities to which they refer. Human beings thus contribute a special class of event to the world: actions. P-predicates formulate actions for people to perform which are events that would not otherwise have occurred. The speaker of a language can formulate active P-predicates for himself to perform such as, 'I shall lure her into the bedroom.' Active P-predicates are the spring boards of the actions they describe.

EXPERIENTIAL P-PREDICATES

These ascribe experience to people: sensations, emotions, feelings. They also ascribe memory and perception. At first glance it would appear that such things are subjective and locked away inside each person. This may or may not be true, but the language used for describing and expressing this experience cannot, logically, be supported by such subjective material. This is because, as Wittgenstein has shown, it must be possible to check the use of a word against what is publicly accessible. For example, the fact that I am using the word 'tree' in the same way as you is ultimately verifiable by pointing to a tree. There is an external point of reference against which we can check the use of the word. Where the language of experience is concerned it would appear as if the 'object' against which the use of a word might be checked is not publicly accessible, but locked away inside each person. This means that if the use of the word 'tired' could only be checked against the 'inner' experience there would be no means of knowing whether I, you, or any two people, were using the word in the same way. So, Wittgenstein argued, the word must be validated in some other way. He suggested that, like the rest of language, it is supported in use by publicly accessible criteria. Where I use the word 'tired' of someone, others will accept that use if there are certain 'symptoms' which are taken to support the use of the word - dark rings under the eyes, closing of the eyes, stumbling speech, slow movements, etc. The ascription of tiredness to some-one will be acceptable also if others know that he has been awake for twenty-four hours. Such publicly accessible phenomena support the use of the word 'tired'.

Kenny (1963, p.67) has suggested that there are three different sorts of link with the world that support the use of experience-ascribing words and statements. The first, as in the last paragraph, is with the 'symptom-atology' of the experience. The use of the word 'tired' needs the support of bodily manifestations of tiredness; 'anger' needs the support of the bodily signs of anger - raised voice, staring eyes, clenched fist, etc. The second link is with circumstances. Someone can validly be said to be angry if it is clear that he has something or someone to be angry with. Wittgenstein (1968, sec.476) made it clear that emotions have objects in a person's environment. So we are angry with someone, rejoice at something, are guilty about something, etc. The third link is with action. If a person is said to be angry he might be expected to do something about it - hit someone, shout at him, etc. If someone is tired he might be expected to make efforts to find somewhere to sleep for an uninterrupted period. If someone is frightened he might be expected to run away from or attack the object of his fear.

Not all these links have to be apparent for the word to be validly used. It might be possible fairly to describe someone as angry if he showed no bodily symptoms, took no action, but it was clear that his circumstances were such as to provide him with an object of anger: someone had just insulted him.

It is the self-ascription of experiential P-predicates that gives rise to the greatest difficulties. As has been shown, P-predicates are not self-ascribed on the basis of observation. I know that I am angry without having to observe my own symptoms, circumstances and actions. If I say, 'I am angry', this is not only a description, it is, as Wittgenstein, Kenny, Malcolm and others have suggested, an expression of anger. It is neither true nor false; it is just part of my angry behaviour. It is part of the evidence on which other people decide whether the words are appropriate as a description. To understand this it is necessary to go back to the learning of language. When a child is angry he screams and cries and shakes his arms and stamps his feet. This Wittgenstein would have described as the natural expression of anger. As a child learns language, he learns to add the words 'I am angry' to his angry behaviour.

As words, however, 'I am angry' remain part of a linguistic system and convey meaning. The words cannot be totally assimilated to natural behaviour. As well as expressing anger, they ascribe it to me. As an expression of anger they are always, as Kenny says (1971, pp.204ff.), replaceable by natural behaviour. Ordinary descriptions of reality are not replaceable by behaviour in this way.

'I am going for a walk' is not an expression of

walking, or replaceable by natural behaviour. As a
description, a self-ascribed experiential P-predicate
must be logically distinct from what it describes; as an
expression it is part of what it describes. It always
retains this ambiguous character. This leads Kenny to
maintain that there is an ultimate privileged access to
experience. If all the links with the environment are
missing and yet someone honestly persists in saying he is
angry it must be accepted that he is. This is because to
others the words are a description of anger and to himself
they are both a description and an expression.

When someone says what he is angry with we know something about the sort of anger he is experiencing, for
anger with a naughty child is different from anger at
being cheated at cards. The links with the environment
thus specify what sort of emotion we are experiencing as
well as being the criteria for the use of emotional words.
As each one of us is speaker as well as hearer, we define
our emotions for ourselves as well as others in this way.

There is also a difference between the object and the
cause of an emotion. A child's fear of a fire is not
caused by the fire but by his previous experience. The
fire is the object of fear; previous experience the cause.
Sometimes, of course, the object can be the cause as well.
Kenny suggests that it is always possible to work out
whether a sentence refers to the object or cause of an
emotion by deciding whether or not the person would have
felt as he did without believing the object of his
emotions to exist. For example: 'I was angry because of
the way he spoke' is a sentence in which the person would
not have been angry had he not been spoken to in a
certain way. So the other's words are an object as well
as a cause. Very often we try to find the object of
someone's fear before we find the cause. We have to find
what sort of fear it is before we can remedy it.

Wanting is a concept that needs a brief mention as it
forms a bridge between experiential and active P-
predicates. It defines a state of consciousness or
experience but is defined in terms of actions. Like other
verbs used in P-predicates it can be defined neither in
terms of 'inner' experience nor yet in terms of behaviour
alone. It has the links with the environment that we have
described earlier. The statement 'I want an ice-cream' is
part of the behaviour by which other people decide whether
to say, 'He wants an ice cream'. Here we must note the
first characteristic of 'wanting': we cannot want without
wanting something. If we do not say what we want people
can quite justifiably say, 'Well, what do you want?'
When I say that I want an ice-cream they assess the

appropriateness of these words by my actions. If I make
no effort to get an ice-cream they may well say, 'I don't
think you really want one; it was just an idle fancy.'
Here I am being told that I am not performing the concept
of 'wanting an ice-cream' in these circumstances but some
other concept. If I want the ice-cream and make efforts
to get it, it must also be clear what counts as getting
it. (This is important for other people's assessment of
my wanting behaviour. Will I only have got what I want if
the ice-cream is in my hand or will it do if it is in the
fridge?) Essential also to a notion of wanting is knowing
what it is wanted for. If I was given the ice-cream but
just sat there with it melting in my hand someone might
well say, 'Well, go on - you said you wanted it - eat it
or don't you want it after all?' If I replied that I did
not know, but that I had just wanted it, people would be
nonplussed; whatever else, it did not appear that I really
wanted the ice-cream. (This is not always so when what is
wanted is some form of human activity. I can want to go
for a walk or to sit down without wanting to do it for any
purpose. Human activities are among the things we
describe as being worth doing in their own right.)

   Although wanting is an experience, we see from the
above description of the concept that it is much more
closely tied to action than experiential P-predicates. As
children, we were trained in the use and performance of
wanting as with other active and experiential P-predicates.
We learned to express ourselves by making use of the fine
distinctions between wanting, idly wishing, day-dreaming,
etc. As we learn language we can, as children, begin to
want a number of things that are language dependent; that
is, we want to perform activities or achieve capacities
or acquire objects that can only be wanted by someone who
can understand their description in language, e.g. telling
a story, asking riddles. Nor can we want to do what we
have no possibility of acquiring the capacity of doing.

   While it is in principle true that I must always try to
get what I want, I may from time to time refrain from
doing so because in order to get it I would have to do
something else that I did not want to do such as steal or
deprive someone else, or maybe I am just lazy. It is here
that we may enter into the realm of intention and morality.

THE FIELD OF THE PERSONAL

Strawson emphasises that neither the first-person nor the
third-person use of P-predicates is dominant. He insists
that they are predicates such that their use in the first

and third person is different. Knowing how to use them
involves knowing their use in both ways. And knowing how
to use P-predicates is just part of knowing a language. We
cannot know the one without knowing the other. In this
section we have seen the fundamental importance of persons
as points of reference for language in the world. It is
the person who uses the language to refer to other
material objects and events and processes. The development and use of language depends on the existence of a
society of others capable of recognising things, events
and processes as the same. No individual could use
language or P-predicates without the presence of others to
support him in that use. When P-predicates are being used
he needs other people - another person - to confirm his
use. Our existence as individual people depends on the
existence of other persons to confirm our use of personal
concepts. Similarly, others need us to confirm them as
persons. When we use ordinary language and P-predicates
we are stepping into that area of rule-following and rule-
creating behaviour in which we act as persons ourselves;
in which we invoke others as persons; and in which we ourselves are invoked as persons. As the rules of chess
invoke pieces of ivory as chessmen, so P-predicates
invoke human beings as persons. It is the rule-following
and rule-creating structure of ordinary language, the use
of which makes us into persons. And the way we use it,
and the way others use it to us, makes us into the sort of
people we individually are. Thus the field of the
personal is a social one. As John McMurray (1961, p.27)
has argued, the field of the personal is the 'I' and the
'You' in a personal relation ascribing P-predicates to
themselves and each other. I cannot be a person without
you.

If we constitute ourselves as people in this way, we
must at the same time characterise ourselves and each
other as people of a certain sort. We perform actions
(active P-predicates) towards each other. Everything we
do has repercussions on other people. So we are
responsible, at least in part, for the experiences of each
other. In that I am, as an individual, the unique
recipient of a sequence of experiences and the initiator
of an equally unique series of actions, I am characterised
by these actions and experiences. Other people give me my
experiences and my reasons for action and are thus, in
part, responsible for my character as a person.

HABITUAL AND INTENTIONAL ACTION

The basic form of an action lies in the language we use:
active P-predicates. As we have seen they specify the
performance to which they apply. However, on any
particular occasion when we use one in description of
someone's behaviour, how are we to know that it is the
action that he is trying to perform? Anscombe (1963) has
pointed out that when asked what he was doing that person
might well reply, 'I don't know. I just was.' With this
reply he admits that what he was doing was an action and
also that it was done without reasons. We should think of
this as an habitual action. Something that the person has
been trained to do and does without thought - habitually.
Getting dressed in the morning, combing one's hair, going
for a walk before breakfast are all habitual actions that
are performed for no particular purpose each time they
occur. All that the person would say if asked is, 'I
don't really know. I just do.' They are actions or fall
under the description of action in that if the person had
not done what he did they would not have happened. He is
performing the concept, even if automatically. It does,
however, have to be an action that he performs, something
that can be ascribed to persons in the form of an active
P-predicate.
 However, assuming that the person does know what he is
trying to do, how do we know which of perhaps a number of
possible descriptions is the applicable one? If we ask
him, we may find that he is doing several things. The
span of an action is the intention with which a sequence
of things is done. Let us take an example. I see a man
moving his arm, held straight at the elbow, up over his
head and down again in a circular movement. I say:
 (a) 'What are you doing?' and he replies, 'Swinging my
      arm.' (This is almost an offensive reply as it is
      obvious that this is what he is doing assuming him
      to be capable of action at all.)
 (b) 'Why are you swinging your arm', and I get the
      answer, 'To test my injured elbow.' I then inquire:
 (c) 'Why are you testing your injured elbow?', and am
      told, 'To see if I can practise my bowling.'
 (d) 'Why do you want to practise your bowling?'
      'To prepare for the opening spell of bowling.'
 (e) 'Why do you want to prepare for the opening spell?'
      'So that we can win the match.'
Answers (a)-(d) all describe what the man was doing in
moving his arm. They could all equally well have been
given in answer to question (a). But answer (e) does not
describe what the man was doing in swinging his arm. The

sequence of truthful answers to question (a) is broken at
this point. Winning the match would be a consequence of
what he was doing and could have been a reason for doing
what he did but it is not what he was doing.

Answer (d) is the intention with which the man was
swinging his arm. The sequence (a)-(d) are statements of
intention and each valid as an answer to question (a).
They are not synonymous however. Each one describes
slightly wider circumstances and is, therefore, dependent
on the previous answer.

Each step towards (d) is a means to that end. There
could be more steps that would have been elicited by
further questions.

Intentional action has close connection with 'wanting',
discussed above. The intention with which someone does
something is what that person wants, either for its own
sake or because it is necessary in order to achieve
something else. In this case the actions the person
performed achieved a state of preparedness which was
essential if the match was to be won. The state of
preparedness was what the man wanted to achieve. The
actions he took indicated what he really wanted to do,
because a person cannot be said to 'want' unless he
generally tries to get. What he wanted it for is also
evident - to win the match. Intentional action is always
directed towards what someone wants in this way, even
though it may not be explicitly stated.

A person knows what he is doing in doing something else
on grounds other than observation. This is because he is
performing an active P-predicate. He knows that he is
swinging his arm or practising. He also knows the
intention with which he does something on grounds other
than observation. In the first place this is because what
he is trying to achieve is something that he wants, be it
an object, a state or an activity. As has been said, the
person himself is the final judge of what he wants.
Others may make suggestions, but it is he who decides
whether what they suggest is what he wants, or makes what
they suggest what he wants. Second, if he wants something
he must generally do something to get it (otherwise he
cannot be said to want it as opposed to wishing for it).
A man is committed to certain actions if the description
of himself as wanting is to be true. So he will know, not
only what each of the actions is, but also what he is
doing in performing them: making it true that, for
example, he wants to be prepared for the opening spell.
Thus the sequence of actions that make up the intentional
span is known as a whole by the person concerned, on
grounds other than observation. This knowledge is also

non-propositional in that I can know what to do in order
to achieve what I want without having to describe it. It
is practical knowledge: knowledge how rather than knowledge that. A housewife knows what she has to do when
she goes shopping without having to be able to say so. A
nurse can show that she knows how to dress a wound by
doing it rather than by describing what she would do,
though the possibility of describing what she does must
exist if her movements are to be actions, i.e. open to the
ascription of active P-predicates. The skill of doing
something is different from the skill of describing what
one is doing.
    Finally, knowledge of intention is infallible. It is
always possible for a person to know what he is trying to
do. He may fail to do it; others may see him as doing
something else because they judge his action without knowledge of his intentions and, maybe, other things. This
does not invalidate his knowledge of what he is trying to
do, only of what in the end he does.
    So the knowledge of an intentional action is non-
observational, non-propositional and infallible.
    Knowledge of intention also has a future reference. A
person can know with all the force of the characteristics
outlined in the above paragraph what he is going to try to
do in the future. This does not mean that he knows what
will happen, for he may not succeed in doing what he sets
out to do, but he knows that he will try and that his
efforts will affect the pattern of the future. This
knowledge of the future must not be confused with predic-
tion. It is not the forecast of an event but the
announcement of a decision.

RATIONAL ACTION

Actions do not just happen, they are performed for reasons.
So actions are rational. Richards (1971) divides actions
and the reasons for which they may be performed into self-
regarding and other-regarding groups. A self-regarding
action is one performed with the agent's interests as the
guiding principle. An other-regarding action is one
performed with the interests of others as its main concern.
Milne (1968, ch.3) argues that rational actions are
performed at four levels. The levels are defined in terms
of the range of circumstances from which the reasons for
the action are drawn. This means that self-regarding
actions are at a lower level (on Milne's scale) because
the reasons supporting them do not take account of others
or society. Self-regarding actions comprise the first two

levels and other-regarding actions the higher (because
more all-embracing) levels.

The first level is that of the utilitarian action. It
is performed to secure a particular self-regarding end.
Milne points out that this end, and the actions taken to
secure it, are subsidiary to more ultimate purposes. An
action is pointless unless it brings about or helps to
bring about some human activity or experience that is
worth while for its own sake; for its intrinsic value.
Activities or experiences can be wanted in themselves and
not for anything. It is these activities or experiences
that prevent an infinite regress in which everything is
wanted or done for something else. Accepting that a
person's immediate ends are thus directed to more ultimate
purposes, expediency is the standard by which the action
is judged. Expediency applies not only to the action he
takes to achieve a particular end but also to that end as
a step toward achieving the more ultimate objective.
Expediency is defined (Milne, 1968, p.84) as 'useful or
politic as opposed to just or right'. It serves, therefore, only to judge an action in relation to an immediate
end. Efficiency is a second standard at this level. It
includes but goes beyond expediency. At any one time a
man has a number of ultimate ends. He has to work out how
best to distribute his time, energy and resources amongst
them. Efficiency is the standard by which the solution to
this problem is judged. Richards (1971, ch.2) sets forth
the Dominance Theory as one of the principles of rational
action. It seems applicable here: given several plans of
action a man should choose that which will secure the
maximum number of desired ends.

The second level of self-regarding action is that which
Milne calls personal well-being. A man has to choose
between ultimate ends at some point. He has to choose
what experience he wants to have; what activities he wants
to engage in, before he sets about the utilitarian
activity for achieving them. His first consideration in
choosing these ultimate ends (if he is not acting at a
higher level) is his safety and security. Prudence is the
lesser standard at this level. Including but going beyond
this is wisdom; the second standard. In choosing, he is
not only prudent as regards his physical safety and
security, he also takes note of his qualities, his likes
and dislikes and his capacities. His decision will
attempt to enhance the quality of his life.

It is Milne's argument that a man is committed to these
standards as a rational being. They are standards that
relate an action to a man's presence in the world as a
persisting material object with the capacity for

experience (the ascription of experiential P-predicates) and action (the ascription of active P-predicates).

The step from self-regarding to other-regarding actions is a rational one. It is Milne's contention that it is rational to be moral (1968, p.91). At the level of personal well-being a person is involved in a whole matrix of relationships and activities. If this breaks down his personal well-being will be harmed. And it will break down if everyone, or even the majority of people, ignores the moral rules, conventions and laws of society and its sub-groups when it suits them. This argument is still, however, a prudential one. It is in a person's interest that other people should be moral and follow the rules and conventions, but it is still open to him to disregard them when he thinks he can get away with it. This position misses the point of the argument. Every person is a member of society (p.94),

> and it is in the interest of his personal well-being
> that its way of life should be maintained. It is
> therefore in the interest of the personal well-being of
> every rational agent that all members of his society
> should respect the claims of morality. But if all
> members of his society are to respect the claims of
> morality, he must do so too.

So if there is ever a conflict between his personal well-being and the claims of morality it is rational for him to make the claims of morality the overriding ones.

Other-regarding actions are those which take into account the presence of others as expressed through society and directly. The first standard at this level Milne describes is that of social morality. In admitting, in principle, the claims of others and society, a person is committed to the notion of social and moral laws and precepts being applied justly, that is on universally applicable criteria - even to himself. This is expressed in the traditional formal principle that like cases should be treated alike (including oneself) and different cases differently. In a society where people are, theoretically, equal as citizens, this entails justifying the ways in which people are treated differently and unequally. This is the principle of social justice, and is the first standard for actions at the level of social morality. In attempting to act at this level, therefore, a person is committed to the possibility of acting against his own best interests.

Milne argues that a principle under which differential treatment may be meted out states that people should be treated in such a way as to enable them to make their best contribution to the social group(s) to which they belong.

These may include the family, a trade union branch, a club, a parent-teacher association, etc. In such groups people are treated differently; such differential treatment should allow each member to make his best contribution to the task of the group. This illustrates the first aspect of the second principle at the level of social morality: that of social responsibility. Such groups are, however, part of a wider society; they pursue policies that have implications for that society and other groups in it. An individual is rationally bound to consider the implications for others of the policy of the group(s) of which he is a member. He has some responsibility for this policy and is involved in carrying it out. Although there are now various world organisations, the largest group of which a person probably feels himself a part is likely to be the nation-state. His task under the second aspect of the principle of social responsibility is therefore to sort out the conflicts of responsibility in which he may be involved through his membership of different groups, family and trade union or work, in the light of national policy.

At the level of social morality people are enmeshed in their society. They are involved in sorting out conflicts of prevailing norms and precepts as they affect them, largely through membership of different groups in society - as a trade unionist a person may have to ponder the call to strike and the implications of such action for his family.   At this level there is no possibility of stepping outside national society and considering whether it is, in itself, an adequate one.

The second level of other-regarding action Milne (1968, ch.7) calls 'critical humanism'. The difficulty with establishing it as a level of rationality is that of moral relativity. If people are to stand outside their society to assess it, what standards are they to use that are independent of all societies? We have seen that P-predicates imply consciousness and help us pick out each other and ourselves as persons. The position at the level of social morality is that the instruments of this conscious reflection are the prevailing values and standards of society. McIntyre (1967, p.95) has pointed out that there are primary and secondary values. Primary values are those without which society would be impossible: deprecation of violence as a means of argument, truth-telling, and promise-keeping. Without an allegiance to these values, co-operation between men is impossible. These are, then, values by which any society can be judged for the likelihood of its continued existence and for the quality of personal life possible. There are, however,

more positive assessments that can be made and which have
a cosmopolitan relevance. As well as being an act, speech
and language are also used to describe reality. Such
descriptions can be true or false. They have a truth
relationship to the world. The sciences give us descriptions of the world that are to be judged in these terms.
The extent to which scientific work is allowed to proceed
and the extent to which a society's values and standards
depend on a wide knowledge based on such scientific work
offers one positive ground for making an assessment of any
society. In harness with this is the necessity for
rational argument in society. Descriptions offered by
scientific work can be formulated into good and bad
arguments; therefore a society can be assessed by the
degree to which it fosters rational argument. Rational
thought is also the basis of rational action and people
act in order to engage in activities or experiences
intrinsically valuable. So the degree to which a society
offers the opportunity of engaging in intrinsically
valuable activities offers a third standard of assessment.
What a society can make available in this direction,
however, depends on its economy, and the sort of economy a
society has directly affects the lives of its citizens.
How a society organises work and production for citizens
is therefore of enormous importance. A fourth standard is
based on the recognition of the person as a centre of
experience. Milne suggests that a society that tolerates
remediable suffering in its members is lacking by the
standards of critical humanism. However, much suffering
is part of the human condition. The extent to which a
society fosters the expression of sympathy amongst its
members is important in estimating the degree to which a
society is fit for human life.
    In brief, then, these are the perspectives that Milne
suggests can be used to assess the extent to which a
society makes viable and enhances personal life. They are
standards which a critical humanist may use in evaluating
his own society. However, the critical humanist lives in
a society which, in some of its aspects, may not conform
to his criteria. He has to live and act in that society.
What are the standards that provide a focus for his
conduct? It is inherent in this account of the person
that whatever significance personal life has must be given
by people themselves. This they do by the actions they
perform and the experiences they give, and make possible
for, each other. So the critical humanist, in his own
activities, 'must make the most of the opportunities in
his individual situation to contribute to the discovery of
intrinsic values and their enjoyment by as many human

beings as possible' and show sympathy and understanding
for the difficulties of other people. He is also
concerned with the nature of his society and the degree to
which it falls shorts of his standards. He is thus
committed to social change, though not, according to
Milne, to the extent of destroying the matrix of relationships and activities on which his and others' personal
well-being depends. The critical humanist may, therefore,
have to accept an unjust social order, do his best to help
those suffering under it and, by living according to his
standards, loosen it up in preparation for social change.
It seems, however, that the extent to which a person must,
logically, accept injustice depends on the nature of the
injustice. If it is such that the safety and well-being
of some citizens are threatened by the matrix of relationships and activities, then, maybe, that matrix should be
challenged. It appears that Milne's theory supports a
more radical view of social change and action than he
adopts.

The type of society for which the critical humanist
works is one in which citizens are given adequate opportunity for realising their potential. Critical humanism
is not, however, a psychological quality. If people are
to rise above the standards and conventions of their
society, that society must make available the educational
opportunity for people to equip themselves intellectually
to adopt the standpoint of critical humanism. If people
realise their potential by engaging in activities
intrinsically worth while, they must have the personal
freedom to discover which such activities are for them.
Not all people will be equally successful in making this
discovery, but there should be equal opportunity for them
to try. People will only have equal opportunity to
pursue their self-realisation in this way if the society
is socially just and responsible, so: 'A society whose
prevailing understanding is adequate will have an open
social order in which all members have equality of status
and therefore adequate opportunities for becoming free
moral agents' (Milne, 1968, p.298). They will then act
with justice and responsibility towards each other.

Whatever opportunities are made available, however,
citizens must use them. A person can be self-determining
at any level of the scale. The rational quality of his
actions will be decided by the level of the scale at which
he conducts himself: 'The higher the level of rational
activity the better the form of human freedom, because the
better the way in which the generic capacity for self-
determination is realised' (Milne, 1968, p.302).

People are committed to some such scale as Milne's

because they are capable of acting for reasons. Rationality, as we have seen, commits people to morality and, at the level of critical humanism, to social change. So the more rational a person is, the more he is going to be concerned about the character and inadequacies of the society in which he lives. It is also clear that each person has a responsibility to encourage such stances in others, for to do so is to facilitate the development of critical humanism and the development of a society that values people who live by its standards. So as rational individuals people are committed not only to conducting themselves at the level of critical humanism which involves fostering social change, but of encouraging others to adopt this level of conduct themselves. In personal relations, therefore, the critical humanist not only helps people to realise their potential through engaging in intrinsically valuable activity, he also helps them to act at the highest possible rational level - that of critical humanism.

CONCLUSION TO CHAPTER 2

The material and personal worlds

Following or changing a rule involves more than simply reflectively recognising something as the same as something else. Where actions are concerned, it involves recognising them as rational actions and showing that one has recognised them as such by doing what counts as the same oneself or confirming them as actions by responding in terms of action oneself. The actions a person performs bring the natural and the personal world together in a complex whole. People do not just act; they perform specific actions that they frame for themselves in P-predicates. In an active P-predicate man's capacity to act is brought together with the world. The personal part of the P-predicate is the active verb and the personal pronoun. This is brought together with the material world as specified by the predicate. What man does is something specific in the 'real' world of material objects. The more that he knows about that material world the more can he achieve and do in it. For example, the more that is known about the effects and nature of a 'stroke' the more appropriate can the patient's actions be. He knows what it is possible for him to do and what is not. He can frame actions for himself to perform what he would not have been able to do without the 'new' technical knowledge. So when he acts a man brings together the personal and the natural world.

When he acts, however, man brings something new into
the world. He is responsible for that class of event that
we call actions. They would not have occurred apart from
his capacity to act and perform that specific action at
that point of time. The personal world that people
inhabit they make for themselves. The P-predicates, the
actions, people perform contribute to a world of meaning
which is the personal world. People make the concepts
real by their performance of them. What a person does
occurs in the world and would not have occurred without
his having done it. It is a class of event which man
alone can generate and out of which the personal world is
made. It is superimposed on the natural world but at the
same time draws the natural world into the logic of its
relations (just as the rules of chess are superimposed on
the natural relations between the 'chessmen'). What is
known about the natural world does not explain away this
personal world. Medical and psychiatric, psychological
and sociological, knowledge does not explain man away.
Rather it provides him with reasons for action. It tells
him about the natural world, including himself, and it
tells him about the consequences of his actions in the
natural world. It is as reason for action that such
knowledge is related to casework practice, not as
explaining away a person's (the client's) capacity to act.
The new knowledge is always being used by someone and,
even if it is used to explain the explainer's use, that
explanation is always being used by yet someone else
whose activity is not explained. What conventional casework theory has done is to endeavour to explain away the
person in terms of some empirically based all-embracing
theory.

Confirmation, description and appropriateness of action

As has been argued, confirmation of rule-following conduct
takes place on different levels. At the primary level one
person confirms for another that he is perceived to be
engaging in some form of rule-following practice, by himself responding in kind and relevantly. This process
confirms that each accepts the other as rule-following and
not making meaningless physical movements. This can take
place in a non-linguistic world. With the advent of
language the scene becomes more complex. In the first
place, speaking is itself an act and has to be confirmed
as correct in itself - the locutionary act (Austin, 1962,
p.94). Once people can speak they can do what they would
otherwise have been unable to do. Whilst a non-speaker

may be able to do some of the things that are described in language, there are actions that are entirely language dependent in that they cannot be performed without the utterance of words: asking, informing, naming, advising, etc. When we learn language we learn to use an instrument that embraces amongst its uses that which constitutes us as persons - the ascription of P-predicates. We can only grasp in action the particular concepts that constitute us as persons if there is the possibility of similar others being present. They confirm that the actions I perform, be they speech acts or the performances that make them true, are the actions I think they are. This they do by responding to my performance in such a way as to show that they have understood me to have done what I thought I had done. Our individual existence as persons depends in principle on other persons being present who can confirm or correct our actions. Language mediates people to each other and the world to all of them.

People do not just act. They perform specific actions. Once the initial confirmation of each other as persons-because-language-users has taken place, the problem of characterising the action arises. This is done through description of what I am doing. You may not see me as doing what I am trying to do. Indeed, I shall fail to do what I am trying to do unless you, and other observers, see me as doing it. You may, incorrigibly, see me as doing something else, in which case I shall fail to do it. Usually this descriptive confirmation is tacit and taken for granted, especially with conventional actions such as signalling or going up stairs. Difficulty may arise with interpersonal actions where it is not clear whether I am, for example, teasing or insulting someone. My intention, what I am doing in doing something else, is also important if the action is to be described adequately. Equally important for description is the response of others - their perceptions of the action. Unless this is made available adequate description is impossible, for their perceptions as well as my intention go to characterise the action.

The process by which a logically adequate and accurate description is made will be detailed in chapter 4. What I want to bring out here are the two stages of (i) primary confirmation, and (ii) description or characterisation of action.

What also needs to be emphasised is the necessity of a positive response from others. Neutrality will not do. Unless they sincerely and honestly contribute their genuine perceptions my action cannot be either adequately or accurately described. This shows the importance of

trust in human relations. Without it the honesty of
response required for the proper characterisation of
action could not occur.

After description there is a third stage of agreement
(or disagreement) about an action. That has to do with
its appropriateness. This raises all sorts of questions
about conformity and morality. Such questions may prevent
agreement about the appropriateness of an action to its
situation.

Milne (1968, pp.191ff.) maintains that personal
identity consists of one's biography as an agent, because
it is as agent that one is numerically distinct and able
to differentiate oneself qualitatively from the world as a
language-user. My identity, therefore, depends on the
adequacy of the characterisation of my actions and this in
turn depends on the sincerity and honesty of those
involved. Unless I can trust them to be so, I can never
be sure that I have done what I wanted to do; without
their confirmation of this I may think that I have
performed an action of one sort, whereas I am thought to
have performed one of another sort. Adequate characterisation might show both to be inaccurate. Over a period
of time I may become quite self-deceived as to the sort of
person I am, the nature of my actions which define me as a
person having never been properly defined. Even if I am
aware of other people's insincerity and thus avoid self-
deception there must remain an insecurity about my sense
of identity since the character of my actions must remain
to some extent obscure. These matters will be explored in
more detail when we are discussing description. But
only if people are honest with each other can actions be
properly characterised. So I cannot be truthful about the
nature of my actions to others if they have not been
honest to me and enabled my actions to be defined. I can
only tell others what I think my actions have been.
People must offer each other some honesty of response for
personal life to be at all possible, let alone rich. Only
as honesty is realised, is co-operation between men
possible. It is only with this co-operation that the
characterisation of action can take place, and with it the
establishment of individual personal identity.

Respect for persons - the personal relationship - is
the highest end an action can have, for it is in personal
relationships that we acquire our sense of personal
identity; we discover what we have done and therefore,
cumulatively, who we are. It is only if everyone
recognises the integrity of personal relationships as an
overriding duty and responsibility while in the pursuit of
his other objectives, that a high quality of personal

existence can be maintained - an existence in which people
know what they have done and experienced; know, therefore,
who they are.   To put one's private objectives above this
duty and responsibility is to threaten not only others
but ultimately oneself, for it undermines the co-operation
between people necessary for the existence of society. If
this happens too often then that aspect of society or
interaction that supports personal identity will break
down.

3

Social casework and its principles

Social casework is notoriously difficult to define. However, Moffett (1968, p.2), Hollis (Roberts and Nee, 1970, pp.36ff.) and other writers emphasise that one of the main objectives of social casework is to bring about an adjustment between the individual client and his situation or environment. The preferred method seems to be by bringing about a change in the individual rather than his circumstances. While his immediate social situation is not ignored, casework writers devote most space to analysis of the individual and a description of methods that can be employed to modify his 'social functioning'. Attention is concentrated on what the individual caseworker can do to help his client; wider society receives comparatively little attention. However, Smalley (1967, ch.6) and Timms (1964, ch.1) give some attention to the relationship between the caseworker and the employing agency. There appear to be two views of this. Social casework is either the service offered by the agency or it is the means by which clients are enabled to make use of the (non-casework) services offered by that and other agencies. Little consideration is given to the agency as an organisation that links the caseworker with wider society. Timms, however, does write that the objectives of the agency can be accepted without question unless they contravene some general human value. 'Agency function' is obviously a concept through which the relations of caseworker and client to society could be illuminated. Scant attention is given to this.

However, Plant (1970, p.34) writes: 'Caseworkers are concerned professionally not with the relationship between man and society as a whole but rather with the way in which social claims and obligations impinge upon a man in the form of a particular social role or nexus of such roles.' Moffett (1968, p.7) remarks that: 'Most of the problems coming to a social caseworker are largely concerned with one or another breakdown in the performance of roles and are actually considered problems because their behaviour goes against the norms of society.' Thus by a 're-adjustment' of the self that he is, in relation to the demands and expectations of the social role he carries, there is an adjustment to society.

There is a similar emphasis in Hollis's and Perlman's problems-solving approach. The caseworker's task is to restore or reinforce the client's ability to deal on his own with the problem rather than to deal with the problem for or with him. It is true that the caseworker does deal with the problem direct when the client's main problem is the 'assaults he is experiencing from circumstances impinging on him'. The caseworker is not concerned with the circumstances as such, but only to the extent that they incommode the client: not with their contribution or otherwise to human life in general, but only with the extent to which they impinge on a particular human life. Thus the individual is the measure of the social worker's concern with circumstances, not the intrinsic merit or otherwise of circumstances themselves.

While the individual is given this importance society is not altogether forgotten for it is the caseworker's task to bring about an adjustment between the client and his social situation. This formulation expresses a distinction fundamental to social casework: that between the individual and society. It is a dichotomy that is assumed by all the authors referred to and underlies the casework principles analysed below. On the one hand there is society; on the other a free self-determining individual.

Another characteristic apparent among the authors referred to (and others) is that of describing both the client and society in functional terms. Concepts such as 'adjustment' and 'social functioning' are frequently employed. This approach seems to imply that the case-worker is dealing with systems whose functioning needs to be brought into harmony or equilibrium.

In the overview at the end of a symposium (Roberts and Nee, 1970), Bernece Simon considers all the theories of casework expounded. She sees them all as based on social-science theories. She writes (p.357): 'The guiding criteria for systematic examination of the theories for practice are consistency and coherence - consistency in the use of a behavioural science base throughout a theory and coherence of the parts into a whole that serves as a guide for practice... one of the aspects of any casework that it is most important to understand is its behavioural science foundations. These foundations portray the theoretician's conception of man and, in turn, exert a profound influence on practice theory.' This quotation, taken from comments on all the theories in the symposium, emphasises that social casework is seen as having a 'behavioural science base'. What still remains undescribed is the relation of this 'base' to practice, though it is recognised as having a 'profound influence'. This 'behavioural base' is scientific as can be seen from the following quotation taken from a discussion of ego-psychology: 'concepts for social casework theory must take into account that these concepts are postulates - hypotheses about individual human development and functioning that have not been validated' (p.366). The concepts of casework treatment depend for their validity on the validity in turn of the empirical findings on which they are based.

This approach to social casework, which is clearly very influential, is that opposed by Ruth Wilkes. It also contradicts what Peter Winch had to say about the methods of the social sciences as compared with the natural sciences. Man and society are considered as mechanisms with which the expert may tinker in order to bring about an 'adjustment'.

The distinction between man and society may have its uses and may reflect the experience of many people. It seems, however, to have so characterised the thinking of the profession as to hamper the study of the complex relationship of man with his society. The dichotomy in its starkest form infers that the individual exists in some natural or ideal way apart from society. The fallacy of such a view has been demonstrated philosophically by McIntyre (1967, p.18) who argues that all men must have grown up in a society; it is impossible to conceive of a 'natural' or 'ideal' man outside any society - a sort of noble savage. Indeed, as the arguments of the last chapter indicate, our existence as individual persons depends on our being members of a speech community and a society.

It has been argued above that caseworkers concentrate their attention on man as an individual - his behaviour and psychological make-up. Society at large and the individual client's social network receive analysis only in so far as they contribute to the development of his behaviour and psychology. What has received little study is the relationship between society, including the immediate social network, and the individual's character

as a person. Where work with persons is concerned, the
relationship between society and the individual is highly
complex, involving a fundamental interdependence, as has
been shown, yet also an independence in which the
individual can see himself and others as totally distinct
from society. Where persons are concerned it is not a
question of 'adjusting systems' to achieve an equilibrium
between the individual and society, but of deciding how to
act in this situation here and now. This is a rational
and moral question about which a decision has to be made
and acted on. There is, further, the question of arriving
at a personal policy or attitude towards society as a
whole. The client is not 'a system' with which to
'tinker' but a person with whom the caseworker can enter
into a rational and moral discussion leading to action.
He may well have his own ideas about the society in which
he lives and his immediate social network. It is a moral
question as to how he involves himself with either. This
is ignored, even denied, by adopting the conventional
casework approach.

An alternative is to consider the client as a citizen.
Raymond Plant (1970, p.46) refers to the modes of
participation in society described by Raymond Williams -
the member, the subject, the exile, the rebel, and the
vagrant - and suggests that the caseworker should have as
his objective that the client be a member of his society -
experience it as a community. This means that he will be
deeply identified with it and find it expressive of his
beliefs and character. His social experience of the
groups, organisations, and institutions of society is such
that he should find them expressive of his ideas and
values. When social experience, rather than adjustment,
becomes the central concept of casework, the caseworker
turns from developing techniques of adjusting people and
modifying their behaviour, to a consideration of society
itself. As Plant suggests, they will come to the
conclusion that there are some societies and sub-cultures
in which it is healthier to participate as a rebel than as
a member, either because the society is too divided to be
experienced as a community or because membership of it is
not conducive to optimum self-realisation in human beings.
The task is to discover in what sort of society which mode
of participation is 'healthy'. Over and above this is the
question as to what sort of society is the optimum one for
human self-realisation. This illuminates an inevitable
uncertainty in casework as an occupation. What the caseworker does will alter with changes in the nature of
society and may on occasion be directed more towards
society than towards the individual.

What a scheme of this sort does is to give equal
attention to society and the individual mode of participation in it. The caseworker is not asked to adjust
systems but to analyse, and help the client to analyse,
society and in the light of this analysis consider modes
of participation in it. Such an approach involves the
client as a rational agent capable of thought and action
in pursuance of a policy. It might be argued that such a
scheme is too general to be of much help to the caseworker
involved in intimate and mundane family problems. What
can be translated from the political level of Plant's
discussion to daily life is, first, the social, ethical
and practical assessment of a social situation, and,
second, the designing of a policy of participation in it.
Inherent in this is the assumption that the client can co-
operate in such activities as a person capable of thought
and action. It assumes that he is capable of understanding his society or groups in it, even if he does not
agree with them. There will be reason to disagree with
Plant later, but he here shows the beginning of a viable
alternative approach to that outlined by the other authors
referred to.

THE CASEWORK RELATIONSHIP

Writers on casework are clear that the relationship they
have with their clients is different from that of the
other helping professions. Felix Biestek (1961, p.19)
writes, 'In surgery, dentistry, and law, for example, a
good interpersonal relationship is desirable for the
perfection of the service, but it is not necessary for the
essence of the service.' Timms (1964, p.91) writes,
'caseworkers have a special interest in the relationship
because it is necessary for the essential fulfillment of
their task and not an "extra" '. The importance of the
relationship seems to arise out of the caseworker's
concentration on changing the individual so that he can
then solve his own problem.
   With the 'relationship' occupying a position of such
importance in the theory and practice of the profession it
is necessary to examine how the profession conceives of
'relationship'. It appears that the business of describing the relationship is of secondary importance. This, in
itself, suggests something very important about the caseworker's concept of relationship. Biestek (1961, Foreword) writes: 'No explanation or definition can do
justice to a living thing; words have a certain coldness,
while relationship has a delightful warmth. Then, too,

social workers are of the belief, and rightly so, that the
skill to establish and maintain a good casework relationship is eminently more important than the ability to
define it.' Timms (1964, p.92) refers to the same point:
'Certainly, some social workers have accepted with
enthusiasm the possibility that one of the most important
aspects of their work cannot be defined.' At first sight
this appears reasonable. What is at stake here is the
capacity of words to describe a relationship. However,
ostensive definition of the casework relationship still
remains open: a teacher could demonstrate what was and
what was not casework to a student by pointing out
instances of it being done (through a one-way screen for
instance).

Hiding behind this reluctance to define is a serious
misconception of the relation of language to the world.
The above quotation from Biestek gives the impression that
a human relationship is something quite separate from the
language which describes it. The task of language appears
to be to define a pre-existing reality. Words are given
an object-designation relationship to the world. This
impression is confirmed by further reading of Biestek
(1961, p.7): 'Practice, in every instance, preceded its
terminology. Skilled social workers were engaged in the
phenomenon which today we call the casework relationship
long before they gave a name to that phenomenon.' Timms
(1968, p.4) mentions that social workers refer to their
relationships with clients as if they 'somehow had a life
of their own which was "beyond" words'. He goes on to
argue that social workers have failed to grasp the importance of language in human relationships. They have the
idea that 'language is dispensable and perhaps that it
ought to be dispensed with in favour of some kind of
communication through feeling'. What he fails to note is
the misconception of the relation of language to the world
which Biestek betrays.

A personal relationship is made up of the interaction
of two (or more) people. The 'Shorter Oxford Dictionary'
defines 'interact' as 'to act reciprocally; to act on each
other'. In terms of our discussion of action, interaction
must consist of the conduct to which people ascribe P-
predicates. Interaction is made up of what people do, for
only people can act and interact. Even if what takes
place is not made explicit, it remains language-dependent,
for people not only ascribe P-predicates to what they do,
they also do that to which P-predicates may be ascribed:
language makes conduct possible. There is a tendency,
however, for caseworkers to talk about interaction and
relationship not in terms of what people do but as the

spontaneous interplay of emotions, attitudes and feelings
as if they had a life of their own. Thus Timms (1964,
p.91) writes: 'A relationship is a system of interacting
feelings and ideas, changing but maintained within certain
boundaries.' Biestek (1961, p.15) writes:

> An interaction, in general, is a back-and-forth move-
> ment of some form of energy between two or more sources
> of energy.... In the casework relationship the inter-
> action consists of the back-and-forth movement of
> attitudes and feelings between the client and the
> worker ... the dynamic interaction of feelings and
> attitudes between the caseworker and the client may
> speed up or slow down even within one interview.

Perlman (1957, p.65) writes:

> Relationship leaps from one person to the other at the
> moment when emotion moves between them ... a charge or
> current of feeling must be experienced between two
> persons. Whether this interaction creates a sense of
> union or antagonism, the two persons are for the time
> "connected" or "related" to each other.

and (p.72):

> A meaningful bond between two persons is actually a
> communication channel operating largely on an un-
> conscious level, and through it many subtle feelings
> and values both emanate and penetrate.

These quotations illustrate Timms's remark that caseworkers see what happens in a relationship as 'beyond' or
'outside' language. It is not only that the persons
concerned may be unaware of their actions and the interaction, but also that the interaction is something that
happens. If this is so relationships cannot properly be
described in terms of action and interaction, for what
happens is logically distinct from what people do. It is
true that people may be unaware of the habitual actions
they perform but if they are actions then the possibility
of their becoming aware of what they are doing must exist.
If interaction is 'beyond' language, as the words and
images of these quotations suggest, then it is not interaction in any ordinary sense of the word that they
describe. Interaction is made up of what people do to and
with each other, not of what happens. The language of
action does not simply describe pre-existing activity; it
is constitutive of action, for P-predicates are not only
ascribed to conduct - people perform actions to which they
know P-predicates can be ascribed.

Biestek makes the point, reinforced by Timms and
Perlman, that casework interaction consists largely of
feelings (whereas the interaction in teaching consists of
ideas and knowledge). In social casework the words

'feelings' and 'emotions' are used synonymously. How can
feelings be what people do? It is the failure of casework
theorists to understand this that is, perhaps, responsible
for the failure adequately to relate language and feeling.
In chapter 2, we saw how the non-verbal expression of
feeling in bodily movements, gesture, tone of voice,
facial expression, etc., was language-dependent. The
physical expression of 'fear' is only fear if it is
expressed non-verbally in such a way as to make the use of
the word 'fear' appropriate. We saw that children are
trained up to this meaningful performance. Fear is thus
grasped in the form of action. We saw, too, that utter-
ances such as 'I am sad' are not straightforward descriptions. They are part of the sadness behaviour. The words
on their own, with no supportive evidence, are sufficient
for a second person to describe the speaker as being sad.
The ascription of emotions in such words is an action in
two ways: as part of the 'performance' of sadness and as a
speech act. The expression and the ascription of feeling
is thus an action (or in the form of an action). The
casework relationship, these writers maintain, is
concerned with feeling. It, therefore, consists of what
people do in the form of conduct constituted by emotional
concepts, and of a mutual effort to arrive at an adequate
description of that emotional conduct.

The misconception of language that casework theorists
evince has some serious consequences. In the first place
it depreciates the attempt to theorise about casework.
For if people were doing casework long before they thought
they were doing it, then there is little point in trying
to conceptualise the relationship. Once it is realised
that language not only refers to events but generates
actions and, therefore, change in the world, then the
importance of conceptualisation is obvious. New concepts
may shape new forms of relationship between people.
Second, if the relationship is created as an instrument
for changing people, its importance as the crucible in
which human beings constitute themselves as persons is
lost. Conceiving of the relationship as an instrument,
the caseworker assesses what he does in the relationship
in terms of its efficiency in changing the client and his
behaviour. What the client says and does is important but
only as evidence of the efficiency or otherwise of the
caseworker's actions.

It was argued in chapter 2 that a personal relationship
is one in which people are the objects of one another's
emotions and actions. To discover what their feelings
are, each requires a confirmatory or corrective response
from the other and maybe help with description. If the

relationship with the client is treated as an instrument
for changing the client's behaviour, then the caseworker
will not be looking for or offering this sort of response,
for he is not primarily concerned about his own or the
client's feelings or actions. What he is concerned about
is the client's behaviour, defined in technical terms, and
what he himself is doing either to reinforce or extin-
guish, for example, certain aspects of it. In using the
relationship as an instrument in this way there is a
subtle depreciation of the client as a person. He is not
treated as an organism as he is by the surgeon, nor yet
fully as behavioural mechanism as he is by the behavioural
psychologist. The caseworker does not relate to him fully
as a person because he is pursuing objectives of his own
in the client's behaviour. The relationship is not fully
personal where the caseworker is concerned. The client
provides evidence of the success or failure of his plans,
not personal confirmation or correction, and description
of what is being felt or done by either of them.

Third, the caseworker may well describe both his and
the client's behaviour in terms of some theory and set his
objectives and assess his success according to that
theory. So while, for instance, the client thinks something he has done has pleased the caseworker, the caseworker sees himself as reinforcing, for example, the
client's assertive behaviour. He is pleased because the
behaviour was assertive (his description) not because the
client had insulted a shopkeeper. This rather crude
example shows how a discontinuity may develop between a
caseworker imbued with some theory and a client who
describes his actions in his own terms.

Fourth, it was argued in chapter 2 that the quality of
a personal relationship depends on the extent to which
honesty is realised within it. Obviously if the caseworker is using the relationship as an instrument as described above, then there may be limitations on the extent
to which he can be honest with the client. The quality of
their personal relationship is also affected by the sort
of discontinuity described in the last paragraph. The
client may be concerned about what he is doing or had
done, what others are doing, what his feelings are, with
questions of right and wrong, etc. To go into such
questions he needs a personal relationship. He may assess
his relationship with the caseworker in personal terms,
but receive little help from the worker who is assessing
the situation technically.

This leads on to the final point. If the caseworker
conceives the relationship as something that happens and
as an instrument, he puts himself, as a specialist, in a

position to claim privileged access to an understanding of
what is going on between him and the client and to the
client. Characterisation in terms of theory takes
precedence over a personal characterisation in terms of
action. This sets up a system of relationships contrary
to those inherent in the use of ordinary language. Thus
there appears to be a contradiction between the claim of
the caseworker to be a professional and at the same time
treat people as people.

How the relationship should be conceived in a personal
approach is probably obvious from the foregoing text. In
the first place it should be seen as the seed-bed of the
primary ethical values as described in the quotations from
Mary Richardson in chapter 1. Through the realisation of
these values in the relationship with the caseworker the
client may be able to recover them in other relationships
(the social situation allowing). Beyond this the caseworker can respond to the client in personal terms, helping to characterise adequately the interaction between
them, thus enriching his sense of identity. This approach
of course necessitates the caseworker abandoning the
specialist pose in the relationship and acting as a
person. It is now possible to see that being a person,
both oneself and to others, is something that can be
learned or something in which sophistication is possible.
Finally, the relationship, if it is not a tool, becomes
the launching pad of co-operative endeavours between the
client and the caseworker. The possibilities of co-
operation will depend upon the quality of the relationship and the degree to which the primary values have found
expression in it and its personal character been
developed.

THE PRINCIPLES OF CASEWORK

All writers are agreed that casework would not be casework
without the principle of 'respect for persons', or 'value
of the individual' in Timms's words. Under this heading
he brings together such concepts as acceptance of the
'whole' person; the person as more than his social roles;
client self-determination; recognition of obligations.
Plant argues that the concepts of individualisation, self-
direction and acceptance are all implied in respect for
persons. Two formal statements of the principles of casework are those of Biestek (1961) and Moffett (1968).
Moffett bases his five principles on Biestek's, reducing
the latter's total of seven to five for convenience.
His list consists of: individualisation; effective

communication of feeling;   acceptance;   client self-
determination;   confidentiality.   I shall take this last
list as a framework.

THE PRINCIPLE OF INDIVIDUALISATION

Writers on casework have traditionally emphasised the
value of the individual (Biestek, 1961, p.25; Perlman,
1957, p.6; Timms, 1964, p.59). Commenting, Plant (1970,
p.9) writes: 'It is the absolute presupposition, so it is
argued, of modern casework that clients are not regarded
as fulfilling certain types and paradigms, but as presenting a particular problem which needs to be considered
against its own particular background.' These references
indicate that caseworkers emphasise the uniqueness of the
individual. This uniqueness is, however, seen in physical
terms. Perlman (1957, p.140), writes:

> as we move from understanding him simply as a human
> being to understanding him as this particular human
> being, we find that with all his general likenesses to
> others, he is as unique as his thumbprint. By nuance
> and fine line and by the particular way his bone and
> spirit are joined, he is born and grows as a person-
> ality different in some ways from every other indivi-
> dual of his family, genus or species.

Now it is undoubtedly true that as a physical organism
called a human being the individual is unique, but it is
not this physical uniqueness that makes him unique as a
person. As was shown at the end of the last chapter, what
constitutes a human being as a unique person is his
biography as an agent. This is based on his capacity to
act and engage in those actions he can ascribe to himself
and others, the possibilities of which are embedded in his
language. So personal individuality resides in the
capacity for action, not physical characteristics.

Hampshire (1958,p.47) argues that in a being capable of
speech and the use of language there is a pre-linguistic
bodily self-consciousness. This bodily self-consciousness
springs from the capacity to do something that is the same
as something else. A baby can copy actions of its own or
its mother's before it has acquired any capacity to speak -
simple arm and face movements for instance. He becomes
'aware' that this is 'my' body and that it is 'I' who is
moving it. It is in performing such actions (pre-
linguistic but language-dependent because copied from
mother's actions) with his body that a baby differentiates
himself from the world, Hampshire argues. This bodily
self-consciousness is nothing like the physically defined

individuality described by Perlman, however.
    Both bodily and personal self-consciousness entail that
a person is aware of himself as the person who is doing
something or experiencing something at any one time. But
he is also aware of himself as a continuously existing
person. It is his body that has moved through a succession of different situations from the moment that he was
born. Where personal self-consciousness is concerned he
is aware of himself as the originator of a unique
succession of acts - including speech acts - and as the
recipient of a series of experiences. Our present
interest in individualisation directs us to the uniqueness
of this continuous bodily presence and the sequence of
actions and experience. Physical uniqueness is weak
ground for respect for persons but agency and what a
person does or could do is better ground. It is his
uniqueness as an agent that distinguishes a person from
other people and the uniqueness of his actions over time
that distinguishes his biography from that of other
people. It is in our individuality as agents that our
personal individuality lies, both in the immediate
situation and over time.
    It is here that we must differ from Timms's (1964,
p.59) formulation in which he describes the client as a
unique constellation of qualities and ends. A man is not
necessarily unique so far as ends are concerned but he is
in the actions he performs, and plans to perform, to
realise them when these are fully described and not given
general labels. When a man says that he is encouraging
his son to read he is ascribing an action to himself that
any father could equally ascribe to himself. It is a
generally applicable ascription. A further description
individualises it: 'I am encouraging my son Oliver to
read by sitting on his bed each night and getting him to
tell me stories. I write them down and then we read them
together. Sometimes he draws pictures of them and writes
the words under them....' A description like this
illuminates the unique circumstances of this particular
example of 'encouraging' by which it differs from other
examples. As for qualities, dispositions, natural
characteristics, skills, abilities and capacities, these
are things that a person has in common with others. It is
the exercise of these qualities, etc., in action (given an
individualistic description) which gives him personal
individuality.
    When he speaks or performs the actions dependent on
language a man makes himself a unique person. Qualities,
natural dispositions, etc., which he may share with others
are devoted to the creation of a unique act; unique as an

event in the world; unique as his action; and unique as
the action of a person with a unique biography of acts,
because it is sometimes performed with these previous
actions in mind (and no other sequence; each personal
sequence of actions making up a personal biography is
unique and contributes to the uniqueness of any new action
if the agent takes his past activities into account as
reason for action).

Individualisation is, however, a principle of casework.
It is something that the caseworker is meant to do. So
far it appears as something that the individual does for
himself. As we have seen, bodily self-consciousness
depends on pre-linguistic movements that can only be
called actions because linguistic ability and self-
consciousness are latent in the individual concerned. And
the mastery and use of language depends on the presence of
a community of others. So we are dependent on others for
our experience of ourselves as people. This immediately
suggests that individualisation cannot be a professional
principle. If, however, it is accepted that the caseworker has a recognised position in society he can be
compared with others who also help people with problems.
It is in comparison with other specialists that the caseworker can claim individualisation as a professional
principle (though not in the way that he does now). In
discussing the casework relationship, it was argued that
in working with people as people the caseworker is
committed to an egalitarian social relationship with the
client in which each contributes to the characterisation
and definition of the relationship between them as
persons, beings of similar status. Only by relating to
someone as a person can the client experience himself as
a person. It is not the primary aim of other specialist
helpers to help the client as a person (and maybe some
would claim that it is not the primary aim of casework
either, but the object here is to see to what extent the
demonstrated concern to treat people as people amongst
caseworkers is compatible with the claim to professional
status). Thus, the psychologist does not enter into an
egalitarian social agreement with the client in
characterising and defining what goes on between them. He
tells the client what is happening in terms of his
specialist criteria. So does the sociologist, the psycho-
analyst, etc. It was argued that what distinguishes a
relationship as personal is the egalitarian social agreement on which the use of ordinary language depends (and
hence our existence as persons). In working with the
client as a person the caseworker must involve him in the
characterisation of action and experience. It is having

this as a primary aim that could differentiate the casework relationship from other professional relationships
and it is this approach which individualises the client so
far as the 'relationship' is concerned, for the client
participates in the characterisation of actions that are
unique because they are his. He does not have to accept
the caseworker's expert and unilateral description of them
in generally applicable terms. Such a description would
simply render the actions as examples of general types and
categories of behaviour. It was argued, however, that in
relating to the client in this way the caseworker was
acting not as a professional but as an ordinary person
exactly similar to the client. If it can be shown that
the caseworker offers a specialist service to the client
in other ways, then less weight is placed on the nature of
the relationship as a defining characteristic of casework
as a professional activity. The relationship with the
client, in that it is personal, can be seen to differ from
that inherent in the approach adopted by other 'human'
specialists, but its importance as a professional activity
is reduced. And the way in which it differs is that it
individualises and personalises the client rather than
percieving him or his behaviour as an example of general
types. Thus in relation to other and collaborating
professions the personal and individualising relationship
offered by the caseworker could be claimed as a characteristic of the profession, though with a significance in his
activities somewhat different from that given it in
conventional accounts.

In discussing the 'relationship' it was argued that the
caseworker is largely concerned with the characterisation
of the interaction between himself and the client. They
are involved in this as equals. The caseworker is also
interested in other relationships in which the client is
involved. Obviously an adequate characterisation of the
interaction in these could only be performed by bringing
the client together with those concerned. However, the
caseworker can at least help the client to give an
accurate and logically adequate description of his actions
in the relationship. In doing this the caseworker will be
involved in inquiries as to the client's intentions and
reasons; as to what he was trying to do. For these are
all-important in characterising an action. In attempting
to help the client characterise his actions, the caseworker is treating him as a person. He is not simply
interested in finding out what happened and then
characterising it himself in terms of some theory (i.e. as
'secondary reinforcement', 'inter-role conflict' or
'counter transference'). In addition, however, it

involves treating the client as the unique and only
source of knowledge in a special personal sense. No book
or theory can tell him what the client is or was trying to
do. No book or theory can justify him in denying that the
client was doing what he said he was trying to do (unless
it tells him about the way in which people deceive,
pretend and dissemble). At the heart of treating people
as people is the necessity of recognising them as the only
source of knowledge about what they are trying to do, what
their plans are, and what they were trying to do in the
past. The attempt to characterise actions necessarily
involves the caseworker in so treating the client. Other
professionals may well be far more interested in what
happened rather than what the client was trying to do, so
the caseworker's interest may here, again, be seen to
individualise the client in comparison with them.

A thoroughgoing characterisation of a client's actions
may well amount to a narrative of his life. This again is
an individualisation of the client. It is in action that
a person differentiates himself from the world as a person,
and a narrative of the actions he has performed, even if
it is restricted to those he thinks most important, is his
biography as an agent; to state that aspect of himself
that is unique and entirely individual. It is more than a
simple narration, however, for in describing the actions
again he may give them new significance in relation to
each other and they will have new significance in relation
to the present, which has changed since last he told the
tale. So any statement of a person's biography
contributes to his sense of identity (which resides in the
actions he has performed) by relating it to the present.
The caseworker, through his interest in the client as a
person and therefore as an agent, individualises him by
enabling him to secure and enrich his sense of identity as
a person. This may well differ from the approach of other
specialists who are interested in his medical or psychiatric history, his behaviour and its relation to the
environment, the roles in which he has found himself
throughout life.

Further, the caseworker's interest in the client's
experience is again an individualising interest. The
client's description of his experience may well lead him
to discover things about himself and will also result in
his finding a new relationship of the past to the ever-
changing present.

There is one last and overall way in which the caseworker's activities are individualising: they contribute
to the person's sense of identity by enriching it and
relating past to present. It is in doing this more than

anything else that he individualises the client, for a description of the client's present situation or his biography in terms of a technical discipline has the effect of alienating the description from his experience as a person, for it is not framed in terms of a description of action or experience (the two sides of personal life). Thus by adopting a personal approach the caseworker is able to make a positive contribution to the client's sense of being an individual person and in comparison with other specialities this could be said to be a professional contribution.

Individualisation takes place in three ways: in the present, through the personal relationship between client and social caseworker in which the caseworker's actions structure the client's experience; in description of the past, in which the client describes and maybe enriches his biography as an individual person; and last, in discussing future action with the client, in which the caseworker is also contributing to his identity as a person.

Individualisation is something that people do for each other as people by means of the social egalitarian agreement necessary for the characterisation of actions and emotions. Only in comparison with other professions or specialities can the caseworker be a professional. The caseworker may be more sophisticated in the use of language but he has no qualitative advantage over the client because he is a professional.

THE PRINCIPLE OF EFFECTIVE COMMUNICATION OF FEELING

Caseworkers are concerned about feeling or emotion both ethically and practically. Ethically they seem to give adequate importance to the expression of feeling (Moffett, 1968, pp.30-1; Biestek, 1961, p.37). The difficulties arise in the practical consideration of feeling. There appear to be three ways in which caseworkers conceive that clients may have problems with their feelings. First, the client may be confronted with a difficult practical problem which arouses such strong feeling in him that he is unable to cope effectively with the problem (Perlman, 1957, p.67). Second, the client may have certain feelings of, for example, apprehension or diffidence about asking for help (Moffett, 1968, pp.18-20). Third, the client's feelings may be the main problem about which he is asking for help (Perlman, 1957, p.55). In discussing the casework relationship it has already been shown that caseworkers suffer from a misconception of the relationship between language and emotional experience. The same

misconception appears here. Timms (1964, p.72) writes:
'the caseworker values the expression of the client's
feelings. He values them because they are aspects of the
client's personality, but also because their expression
helps the client to begin to understand their force and
mode of operation'. The conception behind this is that
the feelings are operating within the client independently
of him. They are forces working within him over which he
cannot have control unless he recognises them for what
they are.

Perlman has a similar conception. She writes (1957,
p.143): 'We often do not know exactly what we feel until
we have communicated it to someone else. We may know that
a store of discomfort is gathered in us, but of what it is
made and how it is confusing and complicating our efforts
to deal with our problems we do not know until we put it
into words.'

The description of feeling is not simply the realisation of a pre-existing thing. It is a creative act.
Whatever existed before the creative act is given a new
existence by being put into language. Just as pieces of
ivory are made into chessmen when they are subject to the
rules of chess, so whatever pre-existed the speech act
assumes completely new dimensions and significance when
described and thereby made subject to the rules of the
form of description used. We do not know what pre-exists
the speech act for it is not in a rule-following and,
therefore, communicable form till subject to language.
What is outside language or language-dependent forms is
unknowable. Thus while something pre-exists the speech
act we cannot know what it is and we certainly cannot talk
of language naming it, for, as we have seen, experiential
concepts are validated by objects (behaviour, symptoms,
situation) other than those they purport to describe
(private, inner, objects). In describing our feelings we
are in fact creating or making ourselves as people, for
without the words we would not have the personal self-
consciousness that the articulation gives us. We would
not be aware of that aspect of experience described, and
that experience would not have existed in just that way
without being so described. The description brings something new into existence. Raymond Williams (1965, p.42)
writes:

This vital descriptive effort - which is not merely a
subsequent effort to describe something known, but
literally a way of seeing new things and new relationships - has often been observed by artists, yet it is
not the activity of artists alone. The same effort is
made not only by scientists and thinkers but also

and necessarily by everyone ... it is in the first
instance to everyman a matter of urgent personal importance to 'describe' his experience because this is
literally a remaking of himself, creative change in his
personal organisation to include and control that
experience. This struggle to remake ourselves - to
change our personal organisation so that we may live in
a proper relation to our environment - is in fact often
painful.

Language offers us not only the opportunity of communication, but also of making and remaking our world of
personal relations and experience.

Because caseworkers conceive the relation of language
to emotions as that of words to object, they misunderstand
the character of emotional concepts and they fail to
realise the creative aspects of speech. By thinking of
emotions as internal forces or processes to which
emotional concepts give a name they arrive at the position
of considering relationships as the interplay of these
forces, as we have seen, and emotions as internal
processes. Now, even were it possible to devise a
language that describes emotions and relationships in this
way it would not be the language in which we understand
ourselves and each other, nor the language through which
we relate to each other. Its use with clients would break
the rule-following foundation of our everyday social life
and experience, and create a 'gap' between the way in
which the caseworker sees things and the way the client
does. In addition, it would be to treat him as less than
a person because the caseworker would not ascribe the
expected personal concepts to him. In ascribing feelings
to the client (and actions) the caseworker maintains with
him the rule-following social contract entailed in the use
of language, that is the use, confirmation and correction
of the concepts on which our everyday life is based and
which give us our experience of the world, of ourselves as
people, and of others. By thinking of language largely as
the naming and describing of forces and processes, casework theorists fail to see the creative aspects of
language. Experiential concepts do not name objects or
processes, even internal ones, as we have seen. They
characterise the personal consciousness of an individual,
how he is feeling - not what process is taking place in
some part of him or his body.

THE PRINCIPLE OF CLIENT SELF-DETERMINATION

This principle is central to social casework (e.g. Perlman, 1957, pp.59-60; Biestek, 1961, pp.101,103; Timms, 1964, pp.60-1). Timms sums up the way in which this principle is used by pointing out that casework writers seem to move from one to another definition of freedom.

We cannot go further without referring to recent discussions of freedom, for these references and the principle of self-determination itself are intimately bound up with the concept of freedom. There are basically two ideas of freedom; the positive and the negative. In the references above, both concepts of freedom are used. Biestek seems to rely on a negative concept of freedom: a caseworker should not wilfully violate a client's freedom. Timms also emphasises the negative idea when he argues that the client should make his own decisions within the casework process and also decide whether he should participate in the process at all; that he should be free to lead the life that he wants to lead. The negative idea of freedom is, thus, freedom from constraint, interference, undue influence and coercion.

The authors referred to also use a positive concept of freedom. Perlman writes that the client should use all his capacities and potentials on his problem and that the client should be helped to use his self-determination in his best welfare. Biestek writes that the innate ability for self-determination in the client should be activated, as well as emphasising the negative aspects of freedom. The positive conception of freedom, as illustrated by these authors, refers to a generic ability to make decisions and exercise a self-direction in working out one's life. So far as caseworkers are concerned their interest in nurturing this quality in their clients seems to be secondary to the process of problem-solving. That is, they are interested in self-direction only to the extent that it is used in the solving of the problem that the client brings. There is, however, some interest in self-realisation. For instance, Perlman says that the client should be helped to determine 'what he shall be', i.e. he should be helped to realise his own potentialities. Biestek writes that the client should be encouraged to use the resources of his own personality. Thus positive freedom leads into self-realisation: a person should be able to realise all the potentialities of his nature.

Milne (1968, p.147) argues that negative and positive freedoms are not alternative points of view. Rather, negative freedom implies positive freedom. People could not be constrained unless they had a personal capacity for

decision and action that could be violated. 'You can be
compelled to do something against your will only if you
already have a will, that is, are able to determine your
conduct for yourself.'

Milne also maintains that there are two sorts of self-
determination. There is what he calls the generic
capacity of self-determination; and there is self-realisation. This term refers to the fruition of a particular
person's gifts and capacities as a result of his
activities and opportunities. In both cases the freedom
referred to is 'internal' in the sense that it is the
property of the individual. Negative freedom is 'external'
in that it is an outside arrangement of affairs reducing
constraint to the minimum. All three conceptions of freedom are used by caseworkers. Both self-determination and
self-realisation are qualities that can be fostered in
people.

Plant (1970, p.27) argues that by espousing a positive
theory of freedom caseworkers have been led to contravene
the conditions for the maintenance of negative freedom. He
shows that the caseworker takes on himself the decision as
to whether those he is helping are capable of self-
determination or not. Perlman writes (1957, pp.59-60)
that the caseworker's concern must be that the client uses
his self-determination to his best welfare. Timms (1964,
p.61) agrees. Plant quotes from the literature illustrat-
ing how caseworkers judge not only the client's capacity
to be self-determining but also 'constructively' self-
determining. For instance they judge unmarried mothers as
unlikely to be able to exercise their self-determination
in their own best interests.

Plant argues that two things follow from this: first,
that if caseworkers are able to make these judgments, they
must be in possession of professional criteria for making
them; second, cases that do not fulfil these criteria are
discounted as examples of self-determination. In other
words the caseworker only admits as self-determining those
acts that fit his definition. Plant maintains that not
even Freud claimed to be in possession of criteria for
assessing whether or not self-determination was being
exercised. The conclusion Plant reaches is that by
espousing a positive theory of freedom the caseworker is
led into breaking the conditions of the negative theory.
In persuading the client to make decisions in what the
caseworker thinks are the client's best interests he uses
undue influence and manipulation in order to 'make the
client do what he thinks is in his (the client's) best
interests.

Plant's (1970, p.29) main contention is that:

The caseworker becomes the authority when a question is
posed about the ability of the client to be self-
directing, and this kind of view could sanction casework influence or even interference in those cases
where a client is supposed not to have taken a real
decision according to the criteria for decision-making
which are given by the casework theorists.

What we are suggesting is that the standards of rationality as described by Milne, to which a person is committed
as a person, constitute neutral criteria. Both client and
caseworker are committed to them as people. They also
form criteria for a positive view of the rationality of an
action in that an action which takes into account all
these standards is more rational than one that does not.
An action performed from the point of view of critical
humanism is more rational because it does not simply
accept the prevailing social values and practices, which
actions at the level of social morality do.

It is important to remember that while an act may be
more or less rational, it is self-determining at whatever
level of rationality it is performed. A person determines
his personal identity when he acts, whether at the level
of 'blindly being and doing' or at the level of critical
humanism. The sort of identity he creates for himself,
however, will obviously be affected by the level at which
he acts. Social caseworkers appear to have confused these
two points. They seem to say that an act is self-
determining only if performed for the very best of reasons
(in their eyes). What they fail to realise is that any
act is self-determining (though behaviour is not).
Unmarried mothers, for instance, are not incapable of
self-determination - only, apparently, from exercising it
in the way caseworkers would wish. By taking the position
they do, social workers make themselves the arbiters of
self-determination.

It is not so much a matter of caseworkers moving from
one definition of freedom to another as their having no
definition at all other than thinking of it vaguely as
some inner capacity that can be activated or remain
dormant. The literature nowhere gives evidence of a
distinction being made between actions and behaviour, nowhere relates self-determination to theories of freedom,
nowhere notes the difference between rationality and self-
determination (but see McDermott, 1975). It is suggested
here that in promoting standards for action such as those
proposed by Milne the caseworker can assist people to act
more rationally without at the same time telling people
what to do or what the goals of their actions should be.
What is asked of clients is that they should consider

their proposed actions by standards to which they, caseworkers, and all other people are committed as persons.

Perlman (1957, pp.59-60) moves in this direction even
though she confuses rationality and self-determination.
She writes of the client's best interests being served if
he can be helped 'to determine what he shall be or do in
contrast to just blindly being or doing'. This suggests
that 'blindly being or doing' is not self-determining. Our
position is that it describes acts at the habitual level,
behaviour that comes under the description of 'action'
(though this depends on the agent agreeing that what has
happened is an action). It is therefore self-determining
and contributes to the person's biography as an agent and
his personal identity. 'Just blindly being or doing' is
rule-following action in that it can be described as an
action; it is doing rather than just behaving. This then
is the base line from which Perlman sees a person's self-
determining capacity developing. She suggests in the
section from which the above quotation was taken that
there is a model of thought and action of which the caseworker must be aware if he is to help the client to think
through, and actively solve, his problem. She continues
(1957, p.60):

(1) The facts that constitute and bear upon the problem
must be ascertained and grasped. Such facts may be of
objective reality and of subjective reaction, of cause
and effect, and of relatedness between the person and
his problem, of the solutions sought and of the actual
means available and so forth. (2) The facts must be
thought about. That is to say, they must be turned
over, probed into and reorganised in the mind -
examined in their relationship to one another, searched
for their significance, viewed in their resemblances to
and differences from like configurations known elsewhere, and connections made between facts of drives and
goals, of obstacles and of aims, and so forth....
(3) Some choice or decision must be made that is the
end result of the consideration of the particular facts
and that affects or has the intent of resolving the
problem. Such a decision may take the form of the
selection of a course of overt action or, more subtly,
of some change in the person's responsive relationship
to the problem. Either conclusion must be tested for
its validity by some action upon the problem.

This model of procedure, she points out, is the same as
the logic of everyday thought. It gets over the difficulty many caseworkers have in using the medical model of
diagnosis and treatment. This is that it does not
sufficiently involve the client in working on his own

problem but sets the caseworker apart as an expert.   In
contrast she sets this everyday method of problem-solving
as an example of the casework process.   What Perlman seems
to be suggesting is that everyday logical procedures of
thought should be the model for the social caseworker's
approach to problems.   It is by using these procedures
that the problem will be solved.   It is also inherent in
her account, that these procedures should be used by the
client for it is the objective of the caseworker that the
client should be helped to solve his own problem.   Perlman
mentions the word 'efficiency' in relation to problem-
solving.   We can thus see how expediency and efficiency
can be the standards of action, and reasons for action,
when a problem has to be solved.   So rather than 'just
being or doing' the client and the caseworker operate at
the level of utilitarian action in Milne's framework.
Moreover it is the caseworker's task to raise the client's
rational performance to this level.

It is, however, insufficient to limit the consideration
of action to the utilitarian level and the standard of
efficiency.   If the caseworker's concern is simply to
raise the efficiency of the client's problem-solving
performance a whole range of problems in relation to goals
and values is left unrecognised.   The scale proposed by
Milne (1968) is cumulative in that the standards of the
lower levels are subsumed in those of the higher.   So
though questions of efficiency may be raised about any
action, they will be subordinated to criteria relating to
personal well-being, justice and the contribution of the
action toward the establishment of a critically humane
society.   A man considering whether or not to go on strike
will, at the level of utilitarian action, have to weigh up
whether such action is most likely to achieve his ends and
how achieving this particular end in this way may affect
his other goals.   Deciding whether or not to go on strike
will involve him in considering the justice of his claim,
perhaps for higher wages, and striking as a method of
achieving it.   The standard of social responsibility will
lead him to examine the effect of his action on the
population and nation as a whole and in particular the
effect on his family and any other groups to which he
belongs.   Each level involves the individual in considering his action in a wider social context.   Finally the
striker should consider the implications of his action not
only within society but as a means to establishing a
society more in keeping with the standards of critical
humanism.   A basic inadequacy of Perlman's position is
that it only considers action from the point of view of
efficiency at the utilitarian level.   So in considering

whether or not to participate in a strike a person has a whole range of considerations beyond that of its efficiency in gaining his objective of higher wages. It is clear that use of this scale and standards does not determine what a person's decision and action should be; it only indicates the criteria by which the decision should be made. What is decided will depend on many things from the general nature of the society downwards. So the scale can be said to be neutral.

The scale proposed by Milne is not culturally relative. The standards of critical humanism establish criteria by which any society may be judged as an environment in which personal life may flourish. Individual people may conduct their lives in conformity with these standards even in societies that do not, as a whole, approach them: honesty and sincerity in personal relationships; the pursuit of social justice; recognition of the facts and adherence to rational argument. This does not mean that individuals should not act with prudence and wisdom in the pursuit of their own well-being or engage in worth-while and self-developing activities; it simply means that these other levels and standards are subsumed under those of critical humanism. This means that in deciding on a course of action a person can take into account criteria of conduct relevant outside his society – or even any society. These criteria are those that would be used in a society suited to personal life and self-realisation, not only for the few but for all.

Actions have goals. Milne (1968, p.83) writes that every action is directed towards making possible some human activity or experience that is worth while for its own sake and not as a step toward some further objective. Dancing, walking, swimming, holding hands, are all things worth doing for their own sake. People engaging in them do not have to give any further explanation of their conduct than: 'I want to.' It is clear that these ulterior ends are themselves subject to moral criteria and may be assessed by Milne's standards. Torturing is reprehensible activity in all situations; other activities are acceptable in some situations and reprehensible in others: one is not supposed to dance (however worth while it is in itself as an activity) on one's mother's newly dug grave ! Actions also have other, more proximate goals. If a person wishes to encourage one child, it is not fair (socially just) to do so by running down his sister. Here, running down the sister is the immediate goal in a plan to achieve the ultimate end of encouraging her brother, e.g. to work harder at school.

Of course not all the actions or 'problem-solving'

activities in which people engage have such implications
at all levels of Milne's scale as the question about going
on strike. Many of the practical problems in which social
workers become involved on behalf of their clients seem
soluble at the level of efficiency. Material problems to
do with the lack of or poor housing, financial problems
resulting from low income, practical problems to do with
child-minding, are examples of the sort of problems
presented by clients. Such problems do, however, have
wider implications for the social worker. As a
professional he is concerned, if he uses Milne's criteria,
at the lack of choice open to the client in such
situations. There is little opportunity to exercise the
generic quality of self-determination. It is not a matter
of the client not having sufficient inner resources and
being incapable of making 'correct' decisions but of the
social situation being so restricting that opportunities
for such decision-making hardly exist. Beyond this,
people in the client's situation have little opportunity
to engage in activities capable of developing their self-
realisation.

The second way in which the caseworker is concerned in
such problems is as a citizen of the same society as the
client. Considerations of justice and some awareness of
what is involved in a society committed to the ideals of
critical humanism should, logically, lead him to engage
in activities to change his (and the client's) society.
Such considerations are ignored if the caseworker is only
involved at the level of rationality described by Perlman.
Use of criteria such as Milne's means that through
involvement with the client as a rational individual the
social worker is involved also with society and its
injustices and with measures necessary to produce, at the
least, justice and at the most a society more closely
approaching the standards of critical humanism. He is
involved in such questions not only as a professional but
morally as a person and citizen. Professionalisation
should not weaken this involvement. It is only by
adopting a model of positive freedom that a social worker
is logically committed to looking at the practical choices
open to the client to exercise his generic capacity for
self-determination. Only positive freedom encourages the
social worker to investigate the opportunities for self-
realisation open to the client. And in doing this he
finds himself committed morally as a citizen to the reform
of the society of which he and the client are both
members. This moral commitment he cannot avoid as a
rational agent and person. His professional status should
not limit this commitment.

It might be argued that the social worker should be
concerned with interpersonal rather than practical
problems. Where self-determination is concerned the
previous chapter illustrated the supreme importance of the
characterisation of action in establishing personal
identity. It is fundamental to self-determination, surely,
that a person should be able to define who he is. If he
is not given the social conditions (in the form of the
proper social relationships) he is unable to do this. So
in interpersonal relations the social worker is committed
to establishing the necessary type of social situation
(and society) for personal identity to be defined. This,
the last chapter showed, depended on the moral values of
honesty and sincerity. Now we see that it is insufficient
for others simply to refrain from interference (negative
freedom). What is needed for the adequate and accurate
description of action is the positive response of others
through the contribution of their perceptions of, and
emotional reactions to, the action of the agent. The
social worker is again committed to these values himself
as a person and rational agent, and to seeing them
realised in society, in his relations with the client, and
in the client's immediate social group.

In attempting to raise the client's rational performance, the caseworker is not increasing his self-
determination. He is, rather, enhancing his identity as a
person. Personal identity is founded on a person's
biography as an agent; therefore the higher the rational
level of his actions the richer will be his identity as a
person. As has been argued, it is rational to be moral
and in being moral a person is committed to the principle
of justice. So the caseworker is doing no more than he
and the client are committed to do as persons when he asks
the client to take into account others when planning his
own actions. And when the caseworker engages in criticism
of society and its institutions he is doing no more than
he and the client should logically do, for critical
humanism is a level of operation they are both committed
to as persons. As a by-product of increasing the client's
rational level of performance, the caseworker may also be
freeing the client from an uncritical acceptance of the
prevailing social morality and the influence of those
around him. This is, maybe, of what the caseworkers to
whom we have referred were thinking when they talked of
encouraging self-determination.

In abandoning self-determination and self-realisation
as objectives of casework, Plant was forced to turn to the
mode of the client's membership of society and suggest
that it was the caseworker's aim that the client should

experience his society as a member. We are now in a
position to suggest that the rules of the 'game' we play
in experiencing ourselves and each other as persons
provide also a logical sequence of standards by which the
contribution any action might make to a person's sense of
identity can be assessed. To these standards all are
committed as people because they are part of the same
'game'. They also provide criteria by which any society
may be judged as a fit environment for human life, so the
critique of society inherent in Plant's thesis is not
lost.

Under this model the task of the social worker is to
encourage rationality rather than foster self-
determination. By helping the client to achieve the most
rational (by Milne's scale) solution to a practical
problem the social worker is also making a contribution to
that client's identity as a person. Because Milne's scale
includes moral and social dimensions, considering a course
of action must, logically, involve a consideration of
society as a whole and the client's immediate social group.
It may, therefore, be rational to engage in activity that
is counter to norms and values prevailing either in wider
society or in the client's immediate social circumstances.
Nor can the social worker remain outside this sort of
activity. As a citizen and person, committed like the
client to rational standards, he must, logically, involve
himself in issues of justice and the promotion of a
society in conformity with the values of critical humanism.
The social worker must be prepared, therefore, to become
involved collectively with clients as citizens in certain
activities. It is surely reprehensible if professional
norms hinder his activity as a rational and moral citizen
and person.

At this point it seems that we must accept Plant's
argument that the principles we have been discussing cannot be professional ones. They describe the way in which
people experience themselves and others as people and cannot therefore be the special property of a profession.
When we discuss casework methods we shall look at this a
little more closely. We must disagree with Plant where
concepts of freedom are concerned. Caseworkers rightly
use a positive concept of freedom but with, apparently,
the unfortunate results described by Plant. This is
because they conceive of freedom or self-determination as
an inner event, as part of the causal sequence producing
behaviour. Because they see it in this way they look only
to the client when assessing his power to perform self-
determining actions. They fail to see that a person must
be self-determining in order to be a person at all. The

question is at which level of rationality he will perform.
In assessing this, attention is directed to the situation
and society rather than individual psychology. Thus the
caseworker's concern that the client should do more than
'just be or do', leads to a concern with society.

The study of these principles has perhaps illustrated
another inadequate dichotomy in casework; that between
self-determination and feelings. Treating a person as a
person entails, as described, grasping a whole structure
of linguistic practice. At the heart of this is treating
other people as self- and other-ascribers of P-predicates,
active and experiential, and as beings capable of the
patterns of conduct generated by P-predicates. There is
thus no division between feeling and action.

The misconception of feelings and of self-determination
that we have seen in casework comes from a misconception
of the relation of language to the world. Caseworkers
fail to realise that our actions as people, and our
experience as people, depend on our ability to grasp
language in speech and that this entails grasping the
rule-following performances dependent on speech. We are
persons only to the extent that we are able to do this.
Doing this depends on maintaining the social contract of
linguistic practice, on following rules along with other
people. No one can be a person on his own. He is dependent on others who follow the same rules as he does. Thus
treating others as persons seems to depend on being
treated as a person oneself - not as a specialist or
professional.

The principle of acceptance is not worthy of separate
status in this analysis as in order for emotions or
actions to be characterised, persons must logically
respond to each other in such a way as to give expression
to what is meant by 'acceptance' in social work parlance
(Plant,1970, p.10).

Of all the principles we listed at the beginning of
this section only confidentiality seems straightforwardly
professional. It is the only one that is not, in itself,
constitutive of being a person. It is something that is
practised between people who are already persons but who
need not be professionals.

THE PROFESSION AND CASEWORK PRINCIPLES

It has been argued that because the principles of casework (other than confidentiality) are constitutive of
being a person, they cannot be professional principles.
However, it was suggested that in comparison with other

professions, they could be seen as at least defining an area of work.

It is usual to divide social-casework problems into two types: the practical or material and the interpersonal or emotional. There is considerable division within the profession (as the quotations from 'The Almoner' illus- trated) as to whether the caseworker should deal with the practical problems of 'welfare' or the emotional problems of relationships. What has been shown above is that issues relating to personal identity underly both approaches, but that these have been obscured by the conceptual confusions of the profession. In dealing with practical problems, it has been argued, the social worker's task is to help the client deal with these as rationally as possible - efficiently, wisely, justly and responsibly. Dealing with the problem in this way contributes to the client's identity as a person, we argued. Where emotions and relationships are concerned we showed that the work of describing emotions and actions also contributed to the client's (or any person's) identity as a person. The difficulty is to state how either a rational approach to problems or description can be a professional activity.

Earlier in this chapter it was suggested that the social worker helped the client or patient as a person and that this distinguished his approach from that of the other helping professions. What is now emerging is that the personal identity is something that needs the appropriate social conditions if it is to flourish. It is also something that is built up through the characteris- ation of action and experience through description and through action at the appropriate level of rationality. There is thus a skill involved in the formulation of intentional and rational action and in the realisation of emotions. Cavell (1971, p.186) puts it thus:

If it is accepted that 'a language' (a natural language) is what native speakers of a language speak, and that speaking a language is a matter of practical mastery, then such questions as 'What should we say if ...?' or 'In what circumstances would we call...?' asked of someone who has mastered the language (for example oneself) is a request for the person to say something about himself, describe what he does. So the different methods are the methods for acquiring self- knowledge.... Perhaps more shocking than any of Freud's or Wittgenstein's particular conclusions is their discovery that knowing oneself is something for which there are methods - something, therefore, that can be taught (though not in obvious ways) and practised.

The social caseworker's task is thus an educational one
fundamentally. It is to teach, 'though not in obvious
ways', people how to describe themselves and their
situation in such a way as to be able to act as rationally
as possible. In the following chapters we shall take this
further.

Szasz (1962) has argued that psychiatry is at fault in
treating as illnesses what are really 'problems of living'
involving morals and values. It has been argued above
that, for people to be able to describe their actions and
emotions, honesty and sincerity must be realised in those
present. Actions and emotions can be adequately characterised only if relevant others make available their
perceptions and responses. This demands honesty and
sincerity. We can now go further than Szasz and specify
what values are necessary in the solving of 'problems of
living' and how they should be realised. The engagement
of the social caseworker in an ethical or moral way thus
runs from the intimacy of situations in which a person is
grappling with the attempt to describe his actions and
experience to a general but no less personally demanding
concern with the character of society as a whole. In what
way is it lacking as an environment for personal life?
What is demanded of him as a person and citizen to improve
it?

At a more mundane level we are now in a position to see
how the social worker's specialist knowledge can be of
benefit to the client. We have seen that the social
worker is not, in a personal approach, seeking to change
the client's behaviour directly, so to speak. He seeks
rather to make available to the client material out of
which he may construct reasons for acting differently than
he would otherwise have done. According to his training
or interests, a social worker may have knowledge of mental
disorder, physical illness and handicap, child-rearing,
etc., which is not general to most citizens. This he can
put at the client's disposal. He may also have detailed
administrative knowledge of the social and other services,
the law, etc.

So there is a professional role for social work. It is
grounded in the argument that being a person is something
that can be taught (however informally) and learned. The
social worker is an educational rather than a therapeutic
agent. He is also committed to the realisation of certain
moral values in himself and in those with whom he works.
Finally he has the practical task of making available
information and advice in the fullest sense (Brooke,
1972), involving where necessary action on behalf of
others. All these points will be examined more fully in
succeeding chapters.

4   Description or diagnosis?

The initial step in the practice of social casework is to
diagnose the problem (some writers such as Hollis (1964)
describe a period of study before the diagnosis is
attempted). The term diagnosis involves an atmosphere of
specialist expertise and professional distance from the
client. It is something that the professional does to the
client. We have seen above that all schools of social
casework adopt a scientific approach to the professional
task. This is true even of the functional schools, though
Smalley (1967, ch.4) advocates a 'growth-oriented
purposive' model of man as opposed to what she perceives
as the static 'mechanistic' models adopted by other
schools.

Bernece Simon (Roberts and Nee, 1970, p.368) argues
that it is the concept of the 'whole man' - man in himself
and in relation to his environment - which is of vital
importance to social casework. The 'whole man', however,
assumes a different shape according to the theory adopted.
Where schools of social casework are concerned (p.387):

> The difference among them was the way in which the
> whole man concept is used for assessment and particu-
> larly for treatment. There seemed to be agreement, in
> discussion, that the concept of the whole man serves as
> a back-drop for both assessment and treatment of a
> segment of the man in interaction with problematic
> phases of his life. The difference seemed to be in how
> wide or narrow a segment is considered appropriate by
> each of the theoreticians. Appropriateness was derived
> from individual definitions of the whole man....

The definition of man and therefore the 'whole man' varies
with the behavioural-science base used by the theoretician but, whatever the definition, it is clear that
the problem situation is diagnosed and treated in
terms of the theory. Even where man is seen as

'purposive' there is no analysis of the personal or
personal help. So a diagnosis of the client is made in
terms of some sociological or psychological theory of man.
This diagnosis is made by the caseworker and replaces the
client's everyday description of his situation. The
social caseworker understands the client in terms of a
conceptual framework, the logical structure of which is
quite foreign to that in which the client conceives of
himself and his situation. It is not simply a matter of
understanding, however, for the social caseworker acts
towards the client in terms of this understanding. The
client may well fail to understand why the caseworker
behaves as he does and become suspicious of him.
    Further, what casework writers seem not to have
discerned is the way in which conventional casework
delineates two problems. There is first the client's
problem which he brings to the agency for help. Second,
there is the casework problem. This is the problem as
formulated by the caseworker. His problem, however, is
different from the client's as the client is part of it.
Thus Hollis wrote: 'The major system to which diagnosis
and treatment are addressed is the person-in-situation
gestalt or configuration....' Perlman (Roberts and Nee,
1970, p.163) writes:
    the inexperienced caseworker can be taught the frame-
    works within which the diagnostic content of social
    casework can best be identified, and the areas for his
    concentrated observation and conclusions. Those areas
    will shift their intensity and relevance; so at
    different times in a case one or another aspect of
    person-in-relation-to-his-problem will be under diag-
    nostic scrutiny.... Ongoing diagnosis designs - or
    should design - ongoing treatment....
There is confusion here since (p.136) Perlman had earlier
written that: 'The problem must be identified by the
person - that is to say, be recognised, named, and placed
in the center of attention.' Maybe 'the problem' develops
into 'the casework problem' as the caseworker takes into
account 'The person's subjective experience of the
problem....'?
    We have seen that all the 'schools' from which
quotations were taken frankly discuss the casework problem.
What seems to happen is that the caseworker refrains from
simply trying to help the client to solve his problem. As
the aim of adjusting the individual to society by means of
a particular agency was formulated, the caseworker grew
increasingly interested in the nature of the client. The
client's problem was really in himself. Psychological and
psychoanalytic theories were used in trying to understand

his inadequacies. Then he was linked to the environment
and social theories were developed to explain his lack of
adjustment to society. The casework problem was then
easily formulated as being to produce an equilibrium
between the client and his immediate social environment.
Concepts of the 'whole man', however framed, while they
may embrace both psychological and social factors, do not
develop a personal approach.

DESCRIPTION

A personal approach to social work starts from the
client's capacity to act, for it is in action that he
constitutes himself the person that he is. It also
emphasises his self-consciousness (entailed by the concept
of action) by encouraging reflection. These two factors
are brought together in reflective description. Whereas a
diagnosis is made by the social caseworker, description is
something that is done by the client - has, logically, to
be done by the client as we shall see.
    Description is a wide-ranging yet fundamental activity.
In the two preceding chapters we have seen what is
involved in the description of action and emotion. We saw
that the adequate description of action demanded the
honest and positive response of relevant others so that
the person describing his action could discover whether or
not he had succeeded in doing what he was trying to do. We
saw how emotions are realised through description -
description of their objects, their 'symptoms' or bodily
expressions, and the conduct to which they gave rise. We
saw how actions could be characterised as more or less
rational. All this descriptive work is done by the client
and in doing it he enhances his identity as a person, for
in characterising his actions and emotions he characterises himself as a person. This is why, as Raymond
Williams argued, description is such a fundamentally
important activity.
    There is a further dimension to description. In
discussing pain, Wittgenstein (1968, sec.244) argued that
words replaced the physical expression of pain such as
crying. Kenny, as we saw in the last chapter, conceived
of the language of emotion as being 'added to' the
physical expression of emotion as a further means of
expression. This was in addition to the descriptive role
of language vis-a-vis emotion. Wittgenstein also maintained (1968, sec.305) that he was not denying inner
experience, only that it could validate the use of
language. Now tears, certain bodily positions and move-

ments in a certain situation can express pain or grief. Like words, they symbolise the emotion as well as express- ing it. People are taught to express their emotions through such symbolic bodily manifestations, as well as being taught to express them in language. People, as Cavell remarks (1958), learn language and the world together. As the child learns the use of the word 'fear', he learns in what situation and to what behaviour in others it can be ascribed. He learns to use the word as part of his expression of fear in such a way that others would use it to describe his emotion and accept the word in his mouth, not only as an expression of, but also as an ascription of, fear to himself. The mode of expression communicates to others as well as to the subject what the emotion is. So emotions may be symbolised, expressed, and communicated not only in language but bodily - and people can be assisted to express and symbolise them so. Many psychotherapeutic techniques of the late 1960s and the 1970s can be viewed as enabling people to express, symbol- ise and describe their emotions and experience in these physical ways. The term 'non-verbal communication' is frequently used of what people convey to each other by tone of voice, posture, gesture, etc. We can now see that while the symbolism is non-verbal, it is language- dependent and learned with language. Abreactive psycho- therapeutic techniques help people to express and realise their emotions in symbolic, language-dependent but non- linguistic forms: crying, fist-shaking, laughing, etc. Arthur Janov (1973, p.88), for example, writes: 'A woman kept having the feeling that she was uncomfortable and unhappy and didn't know why. She kept wailing, "I can't cry, I can't cry". Suddenly she relived an experience and tears gushed out of her eyes....' The tears here seem to express and describe her unhappiness. Different psycho- logical theories underlie these therapeutic techniques. I am not either accepting or rejecting them. All I wish to do is to point out that abreactive techniques fit into descriptive activity.

With description the social caseworker's task is to guide and encourage the client's activity. If the client is trying to describe his emotions, the social caseworker can help him to follow the logical requirements mentioned in chapter 2. This means directing the client's attention to the bodily symptoms - the lump in the throat; the circumstances - including the object of the emotion - what he was angry about; and what he did - Did he cry and then ask his wife for the Kleenex? Did he leave the room to sob in the bedroom? etc. There is also the question of how the person feels now about the situation he describes,

its present significance. To the above directions for
description can be added physical expression: the social
worker can help the client to express his grief in tears,
his disillusion in laughter, his anger through shouting,
etc. Some indication as to how this can be done is
available from the Reciprocal Counselling movement
(Jackins, 1965, 1970). A distinction should be made, however, between the psychological theories underlying this
and other schools of counselling and the methods (often
common to different schools) used. Methods involving the
physical expression of emotion result in that emotion
being symbolised in a meaningful form, made comprehensible
both to others and its owner. The physical expression of
emotion is a symbolic/descriptive activity.

The logical criteria for the description of emotion set
forth above and derived from Kenny (1963, pp.67ff.) apply
to all persons intent on describing their emotions. In
encouraging the client (a person) to follow them, the
social worker is doing no more than he should, logically,
require of himself and anyone else. We saw in chapter 3
that it is possible to learn to be a person. While the
social worker does not make a diagnosis of the client's
psychological condition, he can help him to learn a way of
enhancing his identity as a person - by realising his
emotions through description. What the social worker does
is to make explicit, and help the client to engage in, an
activity applicable to all people as people. His skill
lies in his knowledge of what is involved in being a
person.

Cavell (1971, pp.188-9) remarks that 'feelings ... are
expressed in speech and conduct generally and the (actual,
empirical) problem of the knowledge of oneself and of
others is set by the multiple and subtle distortions of
their expression'. This distortion may be avoided to some
extent by fulfilling the logical requirements set out
above. The distortion of emotion in conduct occurs, in
the first instance, through the actions people may take
such as restraining their emotions, pretending they feel
other than they do, avoiding the expression of emotion,
etc. At one level people may be very aware of what they
are doing when they do such things. At another level,
they may be quite unaware of the way in which they are
restraining their emotion because they enact it quite
habitually. It is these habitual distortions that are,
perhaps, referred to as defence mechanisms by psychoanalysts (Anna Freud, 1937; Laing, 1969, pp.25-6). As
psychologists (Bateson, 1956; Argyle, 1969) have pointed
out, this distortion takes place in a third way when
people say one thing and yet portray something else in

their conduct. Someone may say that he is not sad when
the tears in his eyes and his bowed posture, and maybe his
circumstances, convey quite otherwise. This confuses
others and maybe also the person himself as to what he
actually is feeling. The possibilities of self-deception
are very great.

The discussion of the ways in which emotion may be
distorted in conduct leads us to the description of
action. Before moving on, however, we should remember
Kenny's insistence (1963, p.69) that, given an honest,
undistorted expression of emotion in language, the subject
or client must ultimately be the final authority on his
emotions. This is because words such as 'I am sad',
uttered with no supporting links with circumstances, are
more than descriptive, they are expressive. They are the
only evidence that others have for thinking the speaker
sad. Given honesty and lack of distortion they have to be
accepted, as expressions, as evidence of his sadness.

Given the proviso in the last paragraph, the description of emotion must involve others for, as we saw in the
last chapter, emotions are expressed in the form of an
action. They are part of the rule-following activity that
makes human beings into persons (just as the rules of
chess make pieces of ivory into chessmen). So if a person
is trying to describe how she felt on some past occasion
it is useful, if not necessary, to have others who were
involved present. If, for instance, a mother is describing an incident at the breakfast table and says that she
was irritated because her husband kept reading the news-
paper while she was talking to him, her son or husband
might be able to tell her that she looked more than
irritated, she was flaming mad. She went bright red,
shook all over and took hold of a tea cup as if to throw
it at him. If the mother is talking to the social worker
on her own, he may eventually be able to arrive at an
understanding that would quickly have been given him if
either husband or son had been present, by getting her to
go into detailed description of the whole incident
including her bodily symptoms (flushing), and actions
(grasping the tea cup). Through such a description the
mother may arrive at an understanding that she was more
than irritated. This indicates two things for social
workers interested in adopting a personal approach. First,
the importance for the client of describing emotions in
the presence of relevant others whose positive contribution can enable the client accurately to realise her
emotions in description. In highly emotionally charged
situations there are obviously skills involved in
conducting such meetings so that the client is able to

describe her emotions (Jones and Pollak, 1968). Second, when it is not possible to work with relevant others the importance of detailed individual description emerges.

In a family situation such as the one above, moral issues are well to the fore. The mother can only arrive at a clear understanding of her emotions if she gets an honest response from the others and if she, too, is honest. She will remain convinced that she was simply irritated (and act in that belief in future) unless her husband and son present her with the evidence that she was very angry. Given the evidence she must logically accept that the rule-following conduct she was engaged in was anger, not irritation. It is of crucial importance that people do act with honesty in such situations for people's identity as persons depends on it. Only if husband or son describe what they actually saw in some detail will it be possible to arrive at a decision as to whether the mother was angry or irritated.

So the opportunity for them to describe their perceptions must be provided. And it is obviously important that they use this opportunity with honesty, not saying what they know to be untrue or withholding information out of fear, deference, etc. The mother's self-knowledge and identity as a person depend on this.

After all the evidence has been contributed, there is the matter of deciding whether the mother was actually irritated or angry. In deciding this, the egalitarian nature of the meeting is important. The decision should be made on the evidence and not because, for example, the father's opinion is given more weight than anyone else's. The meeting is of human beings as persons and not in their further roles as father, mother, son, etc. Only if all treat each other as of equal status can it be ensured that an unforced agreement on the evidence will emerge. Here again there are special skills for the social worker in ensuring that rank is not pulled.

In the description of action many of the same criteria apply but the situation is somewhat more complex. This is because actions involve the agent in trying to do something, with the possibility that he may succeed in doing something other than what he was attempting. Where emotions are concerned they are realised in rule-following form and therefore in the form of action, but do not involve people in trying to realise one emotion rather than another. Whatever it was before it was in rule-following form the character of the emotion emerges in description of the social and environmental features surrounding it. Where action is concerned the description must in addition involve what the agent was trying to

do and what others perceived him as doing after they were
aware of what he was attempting. Let us take as an
example a case illustration from a recent work on social
diagnosis (Sainsbury, 1970, p.2).

Mrs A is a 35 year old secretary. She makes an
appointment with a probation officer at the suggestion
of her child's teacher.... She left her husband two
weeks ago following several months of his moodiness and
ill-temper. He accused her frequently of 'being a bad
mother' to their sons, aged 9 and 6. She denies this
and says that the cause of this accusation is a radical
disagreement over her protectiveness towards the
children. The husband has often suggested that she is
making the boys effeminate by her mothering. She feels
that this is nonsense but that her husband is obsessed
by this danger and is therefore over-sensitive to the
slightest physical contact between either parent and
the children. She left home more in despair than
anger. She would not have left the children except
that her mother-in-law was staying on a long visit and
would willingly care for them: 'and I needed time to
think. I can't really think I'm a bad mother, but when
you're told something often enough you start wondering,
don't you?' Asked about the circumstances of her
leaving, she said that she went for a walk one evening
when her husband was particularly moody. She visited a
former school friend (a woman) after walking aimlessly
for a while. When it was time to go home she 'couldn't
face it' and had not returned since except once to
collect some clothes when everyone was out. She supposed this proved that she was a bad mother; she felt
miserable without the children, but not sufficiently so
to return to her husband. On the whole she likes her
mother-in-law, but would feel too ashamed to meet her
again.... She went on at once to say that she tele-
phones her husband daily to ask after the children, and
he allows her to talk to them. She pretends to them
that she is away on holiday and will be back soon; in
one way it feels like a holiday as her friend enjoys
her company.... Neither she nor her husband wants a
divorce, but she would like to make some formal
arrangement for access to the children. Her husband
has said on the telephone that either she should come
back home, or she should stay away from the children
altogether. She does not want a row about this, but
wonders what her rights are....

From this it is not quite clear what sort of action Mrs A
has performed. It is not obvious that she has actually
'left her husband' in the formal sense of the term. Nor

is it obvious that her husband sees her as having left him. There is descriptive work of two sorts to be done here. First, Mrs A needs help in clarifying what it was that she was trying to do. It seems that her move out of the house was at the level of 'just being and doing'. Second, descriptive work is necessary with husband and wife (and maybe children) as to what she has done: has she left her husband, has she simply gone on holiday, has she taken temporary refuge with a friend, etc.?

In sorting out what she was trying to do, Mrs A should attempt a detailed description of her thoughts that day, during the walk and in events that seem to her significant leading up to that day. In going over these events, the social caseworker's role is largely to keep her to the point - the attempt to discover what she was trying to do. While she talks he may make suggestions if he thinks she has said something significant to her (maybe tears appeared when she said it) rather than significant in some theory, and has failed to follow it up. His role is to facilitate as adequate and accurate a description as he can so that she realises what she was trying to do. When this has been achieved (in so far as it can be) the next step is to arrange for a discussion between Mrs A and her husband and maybe her mother-in-law to try to establish what the position is - what she has done. They may well have their own ideas about this but these will have been arrived at without knowledge of what Mrs A was trying to do. Informed of this, they may change their minds. When Mrs A knows of their emotional and practical response to her absence and what they saw her as having done, she may begin to discover whether she has succeeded in doing what she was trying to do. There is a lot of factual material that has to be taken into account - what has been said during the daily telephone calls; the fact of the daily calls in themselves; her return to fetch her clothes, etc. - before what has actually been done can be accurately and adequately characterised.

Action and emotion are inextricably intertwined in a meeting of the sort envisaged here. What was Mr A trying to do when he accused Mrs A of bad mothering? He can only know if he succeeded when he knows what her emotional response was, for this provides part of the evidence on which it can be decided whether he has succeeded in doing what he was trying to do. Then there is Mr A's moodiness and bad temper. Against what is this directed? Does he perceive anyone as doing anything to him that makes him feel as he does? Especially where interpersonal actions are concerned it is extremely difficult to clarify what action has been performed. (When a parent says that he

was encouraging his child he is describing no more than
what he was trying to do. Whether or not he did encourage
his child depends very largely on what the child saw him
as doing.) Mr A may think that Mrs A is trying to 'get
at' him with her accusations about physical contact. His
bad temper may be a response to what he thinks she is
trying to do. Here we enter into Laing's spiral of
perspectives (Laing et al., 1966; Laing, 1970). Where
interpersonal actions are concerned it is vital to obtain
the emotional response and perceptions of others if the
action is to be accurately characterised. Which brings us
back to the importance of honesty.... If the spiral of
perspectives is to be avoided or broken it is essential to
characterise the interpersonal actions and establish them
for what they are - and for this emotions must be
described too. The characterisation of emotion and action
go hand in hand.

Despite the complexity of what appears to be involved
it still seems to be a logical process. This is because
it is a past situation that is under discussion. However,
the dramatis personae are all present here and now and
what they are talking about is themselves. There will be
emotional responses to each other here and now; there will
be interpersonal actions taking place. People will ignore
each other, shout each other down, insult each other,
encourage one against another, etc. They will also be
helpful, kind, sympathetic and understanding. And according to how people feel about each other in the present, so
will the past, however adequately and accurately
characterised, take on new significance. So even as the
past is being described it is acquiring new significance
in relation to the immediate present, which also may need
describing, given the emotions and actions that may be in
evidence.

In order to cope with the complexity and emotionality
of such situations the social worker needs considerable
skill in creating social situations in which description
of emotion and action can take place. He has to ensure,
and is probably trusted by those present to ensure, that
the meeting does not deteriorate into recriminations and
quarrels. Jones and Pollak (1968), as has been mentioned,
have concrete suggestions to make about how a disagreement
between two people could be approached. The literature on
family therapy is replete with suggestions dealing with
other sorts of situation (e.g. Friedman et al., 1965;
Blank et al., 1971; Haley and Hoffman, 1968). In a
personal approach, what the social caseworker has to
remember is that he is creating situations in which people
may do their own descriptive work and work on any problems

that may be described. He is not trying to diagnose the
family according to some theory or manipulate it as a
social system. He is trying to create the social and
moral conditions for the work of description to take
place.

Because description involves honesty (and trust in the
honesty of others) the social worker is also committed to
fostering honesty and trust in the group of people engaged
in description. The Encounter and Humanistic Psychology
movements (Lewis and Streitfeld, 1972, ch.9) have devised
methods of fostering this in people. For one-to-one work
of description the Reciprocal Counselling movement
(Jackins, 1970) offers a range of methods by which a
counsellor may help a client to describe and express his
emotions.

Description can be used in practical situations as
well. If a client is concerned because repairs on her
council house have not been carried out, the importance of
an accurate description is obvious: what the repairs
needed consist of; what she has done, and when, to secure
that the work is done; what were the responses of those
officials she may have seen; etc. To this the social
worker may be able to add anything he knows about the
council housing policy, internal politics in the housing
department, etc. The fact that we are spending less time
on the description of practical situations is not because
it is less important but because it is more straightforward than the description of emotion and action.

The aim of any description is to be as accurate as
possible. A necessary first step in achieving this is to
follow the logical requirements as outlined above. The
difficulties where action and emotion are concerned arise
because a language game different from that in the naming
of publicly accessible objects is involved. As well as
the description of action and emotion the characterisation
of other things that contribute to individual experience
is important. Included should be the description of
sensation, e.g. pain. This follows much the same logical
requirements as emotion except that sensations have no
objects. There should be more concentration on the
bodily symptoms such as location, e.g. 'I have a pain in
my knee. It seems to be behind my knee-cap in the joint'
and nature, e.g. 'It is intermittent, coming in sharp
jabs - when I walk it comes every time I put weight on my
leg.' Conduct is also involved in the description of
sensation, e.g. 'My knee was so painful I had to sit down
all the morning. In the afternoon I kept putting hot
cloths on it.' All this builds up a detailed picture of
the pain. A description of personal experience should

also include all that has happened to a person. For
example, Mrs A should describe what has happened to her in
the period leading up to her departure from home, e.g. her
husband's bad temper, his accusations about her over-
protective mothering, and any other events that seem to
her significant including the practical details as
mentioned in the last paragraph.

This brings us to the importance of the description of
the present significance of what is being described.
Obviously, as the person is describing the past, she is
describing it as it appears to her now, but when she has
finished she may need to turn her attention fully to what
she thinks and feels about it now. For example, what does
Mrs A think about the events of that evening now? And
what is her present feeling and opinion about the people
involved, etc.

All this descriptive work cumulatively characterises a
person's experience, both now and in the past. This is
his experience as a person, his identity as a person -
what he has done, what he has felt both emotionally and in
terms of sensations such as pain, what has happened to him
and what people have done to him.

How does this approach, which emphasises the client
working on and for himself, guided by the social worker,
differ from the traditional diagnostic formulas of casework? Let us examine Sainsbury's description of The
Process of Diagnosis (Sainsbury, 1970, pp.42ff.). We can
agree with his first step that the source of information
is the client. We have seen that one of the first
essentials in treating a person as a person is to
recognise him as the unique source of experiential
information. The second step is for the worker 'to construct descriptive pictures of how certain facts and
feelings inter-act to form the case situation'. In
constructing these pictures the professional works alone.
Sainsbury makes no mention of involving the client at
this point. In the third stage, 'The worker will then
decide which related areas of the client's life and
experiences need more systematic exploration.... It is
important to ensure that the client sees these explorations as relevant....' In both the second and third
steps the caseworker works alone. There is no check,
either scientific or client-based, on the pictures he
constructs or the explorations he carries out. Indeed,
'ensuring' that the client sees the explorations as
relevant suggests that the caseworker should be prepared
to persuade the client that they are so. The fourth step
is to structure the data comprising 'thoughts, feelings,
events, and responses which, to a greater or less degree,

form in the client's mind a coherent pattern or part of
his life'. This 'can sometimes usefully be shared with
the client as part of the process of helping. But shared
activity of this kind should be based on tentative prompt-
ing by the worker, not on the imposition of the worker's
own structures upon the client's perception'. The
diffidence with which the client is introduced into the
helping process indicates how professionally orientated it
is. As we shall see, the concern about imposing structures on the client is related more to preserving
methodological purity than to safeguarding the client from
intellectual violence. Fifth, the caseworker develops
hypotheses 'about the relative probability of the various
structures and about the likely effects of intervention of
different kinds. Hypotheses suggest what might usefully
be discussed in future interviews, both as part of the
helping process and as part of the verification of intervention'. Later (p.47) he writes:

Diagnostic probability rests on the degree of certainty
in the facts themselves, on the objectivity with which
they are perceived, and on the degree of verification
possible both of the facts and of general theories of
explanation ... distinctions must be drawn between what
is known and verified, what is reasonably inferred and
what is guess-work.

Sainsbury appears to conceive of social diagnosis as
the application of general theories of explanation to
individual situations, though he recognises that (p.52):
'Diagnosis rarely satisfies demands for scientific
stringency.' Basing diagnosis on general theories of
explanation cuts across the position we have defined: that
working with people involves accepting the individual
viewpoint. The problem for the person is the situation as
it appears from his point of view. A situation is either
given an individual description (see chapter 2) by the
client or a technical description in terms of a generally
applicable theory or hypothesis. In the first method the
individual·is at the centre of the universe; in the second
he is just part of the situation, described in general
terms.

Perhaps because he sees the situation in this way,
Sainsbury allows little room for the client to participate
in giving meaning to his own situation. It is the caseworker who constructs the descriptive pictures and decides
on the aspects of the situation that need further exploration. The verification of his particular structuring of
the situation or his plans for further exploration or
intervention is by way of 'general theories of explanation'
not by the agreement of the client. Sainsbury is in some

conflict here because he does see it as important that the
client's point of view should be rendered. He writes,
'the caseworker is more concerned with the meaning of the
situation for the client than with scientific objectivity'
(p.52). 'The facts of the situation need ordering
according to their significance for the client, and need
to be understood by the worker not only objectively but
affectively. Past and present facts in a client's life
are, by recall and discussion, subject to affective
redefinition' (p.40). With these quotations, we cannot
but agree. However, the difficulty Sainsbury finds himself in is that of trying to give an individual description and technical and generally applicable description to
a situation at the same time (see chapter 2). These two
sorts of explanation are fundamentally different and lead
to different sorts of intervention, yet Sainsbury uses one
as a check against the other (pp.52-3):

   intuition and speculation, however plausible, often
   fail to provide a valid interpretation of the client's
   meaning, and therefore require testing against a
   continuing and rigorous observation and an awareness of
   alternative theories and explanations of human
   behaviour.... The multiple causation of all important
   human actions must also be recognised.... No single
   theory yet encompasses all these complexities. In
   meeting people's problems, therefore, one may need to
   move from one theory to another, from one set of
   concepts to another, evaluating how far these alternative theories are compatible or incompatible....

It appears quite clearly here that the meaning of a
situation is being weighed against causal theories and
explanations. As we have seen, these types of discourse
are logically separate. The individual and personal
meaning of a situation is not to be found in some general
theory of explanation articulated in terms of causal
relations. The individual description of a situation (see
chapter 2) is its description as seen from the unique
position in time and space of one of the participants in
it - the client. Its individual significance lies in the
relation of this description to the client's previous
history as an agent and recipient of unique experience;
how it fits in with his intentions and his plans for the
future. The causal explanation of a situation is verified
ultimately by the data produced by scientific and repeat-
able experiment and study.

   The mistake Sainsbury makes is to mix two types of
discourse at this particular point. They can be brought
together later but not here. The individual meaning of a
situation cannot be tested against general theories and

explanations of human behaviour.   (We should, however,
note that the description and meaning of a situation
should embrace the facts.)   Even though a situation may be
such as to justify the description of the client as being
in, for example, a state of cognitive dissonance, this
term does not describe his particular feelings, thoughts
or actions.   As a term it is not intended to describe
experience but a situation in which someone's behaviour
may be causally explained in terms of his having two
mutually exclusive concepts in mind.

Thus we must conclude that 'description', in a personal
approach, cannot be merely a prelude to the traditional
starting-point of casework diagnosis.   Description is
logically connected with the ascription of meaning to a
situation and the exploration of significance.   Working
with people as people necessitates ascribing to them
experience and the capacity for action and in this context
description has the various logical characteristics
described.   Description in the first instance details what
it is that a person has done or experienced.   This can
precede the sort of scientific diagnosis advocated by
Sainsbury.   However, if the aim is to work with people as
people a second stage of description can be attempted.
This is the description of the significance of what has
been done to or experienced in the life of the person,
both past and future.   How does the action, the experience,
the whole situation affect the life of the client?   Does
it alter the significance of previous actions and
experience?   Does it alter present intentions or plans for
the future?   In answering questions of this sort self-
learning takes place and possibly changes the client's
sense of identity.   This is why Raymond Williams placed
such an emphasis on the importance of description, and the
pain it can generate.

The way out of Sainsbury's dilemma is to recognise that
in working with people as people description takes the
place of diagnosis, that is description in the two stages
outlined above.   Description at the second stage is of
vital importance for it is this work that integrates past
experience and action, future plans, to the present
experience of the client.   It defines the identity of the
client here and now.   It is the basis on which the next
step should be taken.

Finally, we can see in these quotations how the casework problem emerges out of the client problem.   Sainsbury
writes, in the first of the above quotations, of how
'facts and feelings interact to form the case wituation'.
Later we see how the client's own interpretation and
meaning are supposed to be checked against valid

specialist theory to get a valid specialist understanding of the case situation. Out of diagnosis, therefore, emerges the casework problem rather than a description of the client's problem.

THE DESCRIPTION OF WANTS

Perhaps the most important aspect of description is the description of desires or wants. Wanting, we have seen, has a crucial connection with action. Its description involves both experience and action in that a person can only be said to experience a want at all if he takes action to achieve what he wants (or would, other things being equal; after all, we do not always do what we want). If he does not, his experience is not of wanting but of, for example, idly wishing. A person must always want something; it may be an object; it may be a state of affairs; it may be an experience or activity. In the example taken from Sainsbury, Mrs A appears not to know what she wants. Indeed the experience of some intrinsically worth-while activity must be the ultimate end of all actions, for otherwise what is the point of doing anything? So a description of wanting must involve a person at least in saying what he wants and also how he proposes to get it. We also saw that it must also involve him in saying what counts for him as getting it. The important point here is that if the caseworker credits the client as wanting then he must also treat him as capable of action, for wants cannot be described except in terms of action. The description of wanting is thus a vital bridging activity between the description of static experience and the planning of action. Its importance in the theoretical sphere as a bridge concept between experience and action is paralleled in the practical sphere.
    As with emotions, the subject is the final arbiter of what he wants. The caseworker may suggest to the client that he wants this or that, that his action was a 'cry for help', for instance, but the suggestion can only be validated by the sincere agreement of the client. The caseworker may think that the client is denying what he 'really' wants if he does not agree, but the caseworker cannot ascribe, with certainty, wants to the client on the basis of observation alone, or a theory-based description. If he ascribes wants to the client on the basis of some theory, they are perilously close to needs. Treating the client as a person demands that he be treated as wanting and the description of wants does not allow the caseworker to act as the expert diagnostician. He can only put

suggestions to the client, for his confirmation.

While not involved in the description of wants, wanting leads to moral considerations both in so far as ends are concerned (what is wanted) and also means (action designed to achieve the desired end). So a failure to relate to the client as a person with desires, which he is actively trying to attain, leads to an incomplete treatment of morality both at a theoretical and a practical level, as will appear from the quotations given below.

Wanting is different from needing. According to the two most relevant definitions in the 'Shorter Oxford Dictionary', a need 'is a condition marked by the lack or want of some necessary thing or requiring some necessary aid or addition' and second, 'a necessity arising from the facts or circumstances of the case'. One difference between wanting and needing immediately becomes apparent. As an organism, a human being may lack something - water, food, or warmth perhaps - but not want what he needs. He may not like the taste of something, or have reasons for not wanting to be warmer at that moment. To the extent that human beings are (natural) objects they have needs that can be expertly diagnosed. For the nutritionist to diagnose a shortage of calcium in the body, for the doctor to diagnose measles, no agreement from the patient is logically required. So an approach to the client based on the concept of need allows the caseworker to pose as the expert diagnostician and enables him to avoid the social agreement necessary in the characterisation of wanting and the treatment of a human being as a person. It may be that human beings have psychological needs also: mental capacities need stimulation from the environment for their activation. Stimulation from the speech community is needed if the individual is to learn to speak and enter into the possibilities of personal existence. But it is also possible to describe the individual in terms of psychological drives or processes that have need of satisfaction. Similarly the description of the individual entirely in terms of role performance concentrates attention on the circumstances needed for this performance to take place. In both cases wants are replaced by needs.

A study of the casework literature reveals an analysis of human situation in terms of needs. The failure to distinguish between wants and needs has led to people being treated impersonally. They are perceived and related to as having needs, not wants (though despite what follows below, people may not want what they definitely need as organisms). These needs can be expertly diagnosed. Hollis (1964, p.15) sets out the relevance of Freudian theory to casework: 'It is assumed that the

individual from birth onwards is characterised by certain
sets of drives....'   She does maintain that what the
individual thinks is important, but rather ambiguously:
'the individual does not react to his environment as it
exists, but rather as he sees it, and a host of internal
factors influence his perceptions.   Among these are
primitive thought processes which distort the world of
early childhood' (p.17).   It seems that he reacts to the
world not as he sees it but as coloured or determined by
various psychological forces hypothesised by the theory of
psychoanalysis.   From this position a practice of casework
arises that treats wants as needs.   Margaret Brown ('Case
Conference', February 1964) wrote:

> For instance, the individual who has difficulty in
> establishing satisfactory relationships, who is
> excessively demanding, who lives solely in the present
> and cannot postpone immediate satisfactions for the
> sake of long term gain, and who has a very inaccurate
> perception of reality, has probably experienced
> insecurity in childhood and is likely to need the
> support of a casework relationship which provides ...
> as he becomes capable of greater independence and
> acquires a better understanding of the outside world
> and a capacity to satisfy his needs in socially
> acceptable ways....

I will not comment on all the value judgments in this
quotation.   The point to note is the way in which wants
are classified as the needs created by underlying psychological forces.   The phrases 'excessively demanding' and
'immediate satisfactions' are the ones that dismiss the
presumably expressed wants of the client as symptoms of a
deeper malaise.

Margaret Brown continued by quoting T. A. Ratcliffe,
from whose article ('BJPSW', vol.5, no.1, 1959) we quoted
in chapter 1:

> The most important criterion of assessment (for
> relationship therapy) is the level of emotional and
> social maturity of the client ... in terms of capacity
> for and experience of relationships.... There are many
> clients whose early experience of relationships was so
> unsatisfactory that they were never wholly able to work
> through the initial experience of relationships within
> the family....   This assessment of maturity level, and
> of the role need in the relationship, is often a
> technically difficult task: and it may require a number
> of interviews to complete ... from our observation of
> his present functioning, it is possible to deduce with
> a fair amount of accuracy the nature of his past
> experience, the chief sources of anxiety, and the

adequacy of the defences against this and the stage of
maturity that he has reached.

This makes it quite clear that the need is expertly
assessed by the caseworker entirely in terms of his own
criteria and from 'observation of his present functioning', rather than from discussion and social agreement.
Thus the treatment of wants as needs leads to the caseworker adopting a different approach to the client - one
that is not personal as directed by the concept of wanting, but one that is diagnostic and supposedly expert. The
result of this is that the want is given no detailed
characterisation by description (what exactly is wanted).
Nor is it identified as a want as opposed to an idle wish,
by examining what the client is doing to achieve his
desired aim. Nor are the egalitarian social relations
necessitated by a personal approach established. Instead
the client is characterised by the theory, and his actions
treated as behaviour typical of certain conditions.

Further, the client's behaviour is considered as something
to be modified or his personality something to be changed;
this instead of seeing him as a person capable of action,
with wants and particular actions in mind, the efficiency
and morality of which can be discussed.

In characterising wants, the social worker has first to
ascertain that the client's experience is logically a
want. This he does by encouraging the client to discover
what he is prepared to do to achieve what he says he
wants. With the past experience of wanting, only those
who were with the client in the situation concerned are in
a position to say whether or not he actually wanted whatever it was. There is thus the task of identifying just
what it is or was that the client was experiencing.
Following this is the second-level discussion of the
significance of the experience and actions performed or
proposed in the client's life. In so far as wanting
involves the description of action, questions of morality
are bound to arise, though not at this point when we are
concerned with description alone.

THE SOCIAL WORKER'S TASK IN DESCRIPTION

The role of the professional in description is difficult
to identify. It is essential that he understands the
nature of description in which the client is engaging so
that he can pilot him through it. The 'logic of description' is his objective standard. The professional is
certainly not someone who can tell the client what it was
that he was feeling or doing. The people who are of most

help in this are those who were present at the time. Nor
is he, in a personal approach, someone who makes a technical diagnosis. The professional task at this stage
consists in bringing together those who were present and
examining with them the way in which distortions may have
taken place (if they have). The work of Laing and
Esterson (1971) is an example of this. In their examination of the development of schizophrenia they brought the
members of families together to study how they had mis-
understood the actions they had performed over a period of
years. Here is a small illustration of this (p.35):

When Maya said that her parents put difficulties in the
way of her reading, they amusedly denied this. She
insisted that she had wanted to read the Bible; they
both laughed at the idea that they made this difficult
for her and her father, still laughing, said, 'What do
you want to read the Bible for anyway? You can find
that sort of information much better in other books.'

This shows the way that Maya saw her parents as trying to
stop her reading and their failure to see that this is
what they had been doing. Her father even failed to see
that he was again doing it in the presence of the inter-
viewer. There was thus a complete misunderstanding as to
what sort of action the parents were, and had been,
performing: Maya saw them as stopping her from reading
and they both failed completely to see that that was what
they were doing in her eyes. The professional role here
is simply to bring the members of the family together to
examine what has been happening between them over the
years. All he can do is point to the work that they have
to do in disentangling the knots of misunderstanding that
they have created. The caseworker's task is an educational one in the most informal sense of the word. It is to
show people how to go about this vital work of description. Description is not something that the caseworker
can do for, or with, clients except in so far as he enters
into a description of the feelings between himself and the
client. A part of his task, therefore,consists in bringing together, where this is possible, all those people
concerned in the problem situation for the descriptive
work to be carried out. He arranges situations in which
learning can take place: learning how to carry out an
adequate description; learning about oneself as a person
by carrying out such a description; learning how to
enrich one's sense of personal identity.

As Sainsbury (1970, p.72) points out, the caseworker
has often to decide whether to see the client alone,
whether to see him with the whole family, or whether to
see him with just one or two other members of the family.

He may also decide whether two caseworkers should be
involved separately with different members of the family
or together with all members of the family. What has been
said about the logical requirements of description maps
out some limits to this. From all that has been said
above it might appear that there is little to be said for
the traditional one-to-one interview. Where emotions are
concerned, however, it has some importance. In describing
his feelings, the client is engaging in a special type of
description - his words are not only a description but
also evidence of present feeling. With the help of the
caseworker the client can describe what he feels now and
that description will also be an expression. He may also
give somatic expression/symbolic description of his
feelings, e.g. crying. The caseworker can help him to
make the most logically adequate and most accurate
possible description of his present feelings about some
past situation or absent person or persons. The characterisation of the emotional feelings that the client
actually manifested at the time can only be done with the
help of those who were present. Where actions are
concerned the one-to-one interview is less useful. Only
those present at the time can help the client clarify what
he did. However, the caseworker can help the client
define what he was trying to do and what his reasons and
intentions were. He can also help with a description of
his present feelings about what he was trying to do. All
this contributes to the characterisation of the action and
the situation; also to the client's sense of identity.
Finally, the assessment of the present significance of the
past can take place in the one-to-one situation.

Having said this about the usefulness of the one-to-one
meeting, it must be emphasised that the help a caseworker
can offer a person with problems to do with his feelings
or relationships in the one-to-one situation is restricted
without the help of other family members. This is because
the accurate description of the past action and emotion
must involve them, as argued above: only with their help
can the actions be adequately characterised. Second,
there is the question of the actions performed towards the
client. Both family members and the client are needed for
the description of these too.

If other family members are to be involved in this way,
they must learn to respond adequately as persons themselves with the honesty that alone enables a logically
adequate and accurate description to take place. Thus the
caseworker becomes concerned with the personal interaction
in the family as a whole at least so far as the relations
with the client are concerned. A further reason for

involving other members of the family comes to mind when we remember that the caseworker is simply acting as a person himself. He is doing no more than other members of the family could do for themselves if shown how; that is, to relate to each other in such a way as to ensure that actions and experiences of all family members are adequately characterised and thus secure the sense of identity of each family member. As has been argued, essential to this are relationships facilitating an egalitarian social agreement. The work of Laing and Esterson (e.g. 1971, p.36) shows how this can be done and what can happen if it is not. The task of the caseworker is thus that of informal educator.

It must be remembered that all those concerned in the characterisation of action and experience will describe it in terms of the situation in which it took place. So it is vital that there should be genuine agreement as to what the situation was. In a family this may be clear, but Laing (1967) has forcefully described how the views of the schizophrenic, the depressed and the deprived, as to the nature of situations may be at variance with, but just as valid as, those of others - even within the same family. When this happens only a lengthy process of disentanglement will make it possible for family members to comprehend how they came to see situations in which they were physically present so differently. Not only disentanglement may take place but adequate and accurate description for the first time (unless there is a difference of view based on clearly described attitudes). As actions become characterised so situations will be changed and with this change subsequent actions and experience can be shown to be based on inadequate understanding of what the situation was.

It has been emphasised that in working with people as people the caseworker must himself act as a person. This goes for the others concerned. A father should not use his position as father to tell others what it is they are feeling or felt, what they are doing or did, what they are thinking or thought. If he does any of these things he is relating to them as a father rather than as a person. The adequacy of the descriptive work depends on people relating as people (that is of equal status), for only if the social relations inherent in the proper use of ordinary language are followed can individual people grasp themselves as the people they are - characterise themselves as persons. For in being persons we are persons of a certain sort and we can only find out what sort if the acts we perform and the emotions we have are adequately described. And the description is adequate only if it is logically

sufficient and the agreement on which it is based is an
agreement between equals and not a compromise or an agreement involving the submission of the person concerned or
his manipulation into a false or pseudo agreement. Thus a
major task of the social worker is to ensure that people
in a family meeting to describe action and feeling, meet
as equals and that any definitions and descriptions made
are the result of a true agreement between all concerned.

The logical requirements of description constitute a
neutral standard that the social caseworker may use in his
work. Such a standard is intimately related to the
client's identity as a person because in characterising
his emotions and actions the client is enhancing his
identity as a person. Description is also linked with the
notion of the person because it is something that a person
does for himself, rather than, as in diagnosis, having it
done to him. Finally, description involves the fundamental value of honesty. It can only take place properly
if people are honest and sincere with each other. Without
honesty, as has been said, society and personal existence
as such would be impossible. The social worker in a
personal approach is thus committed to the promotion of
honesty between people, especially where the problem being
faced is an interpersonal one (as with Mr and Mrs A).

Descriptive work like this obviously affects people's
beliefs and opinions about each other. Where beliefs and
opinions are concerned, language has a true/false
relationship to the world. In characterising action,
experience and situations it becomes possible to hold
more accurate opinions and beliefs about them.

There is one last important point to be made. It is
one that, like the description of wants, leads into the
discussion of action. No description is neutral. It is
related to the purpose of the agent. What, in a situation,
is described is related to this purpose. An appropriate,
a sufficient, description of a piece of land by a scout
master to a troop leader organising a trek will be quite
different from a description of that same piece of land by
a botanist, a military leader considering an infantry
attack, or a poet. Each, however, will attempt a description sufficient for his purposes. Only the results will
indicate whether that description was adequate. So what
someone wants will affect what he describes. If Mrs A
wants some sort of emotional help the adequate and
accurate description of her situation should involve
detailed characterisation of the actions and experience of
those involved. If she wants a divorce, the description
will involve those factors relevant to achieving this.
As what someone wants emerges from a description it will

affect how that description continues. So the social
caseworker should encourage - if it is necessary - a
person to clarify their desires as soon as possible in the
descriptive process. This may be difficult, for in
situations such as Mrs A's what is wanted emerges only
gradually and through the description. If, however, she
is aware that she is searching for what she wants she can
use the description for this purpose. The social caseworker should help her to do this.

DESCRIPTION AND FAMILY THERAPY

It should be apparent from the above that in a personal
approach much of the social work takes place in a family
(or group) setting. So personal social work is almost by
definition family work. The task is not, as Scherz
(Roberts and Nee, 1970), suggests, to diagnose the family
communication system and then involve the family members
in changing it where necessary. In a personal approach
the first step is the description, which has to be done by
family members, of what they have been and are doing to
each other. It is not a matter of characterising actions
haphazardly. Those which are thought to be of current
significance by the client or some other family member are
the subject of the group's attention. As a member of the
group, though not of the family, the caseworker has to
argue, along with the others, why one situation should be
characterised rather than another. Maybe an agenda can
quite formally be made. The starting-point is thus always
the present feeling and thought of family members. It is
what, from the past, is of significance to them now, in
the present, that is discussed and characterised. As
explained above, the characterisation of action and
emotion go together.
    The second stage of description is to relate the (re-
described) past to the present and help family members to
describe what they now think and feel about the past
incident on which they had been working, what they now
think and feel about the other members who were involved.
This engages them in reconstructing the significance of
the past and of other members of the family both in the
past and in the present.
    The third phase of the descriptive work covers people's
beliefs about each other. A mark of a belief is its
continuance over time. This distinguishes it from an
opinion or passing thought, which does not necessarily
have to have this continuity. Beliefs also inform a
person's actions. What he believes about the world and

other people forms part of the grounds for his acting in
the way he does. The reorganising of experience and
action through description should lead to some of a
person's beliefs being shown to be false or partly so. One
family member's beliefs about another may change (or
should change) as he finds that the actions that he
thought that that person had performed had not in fact
been performed. As beliefs are held over a long period of
time and as they also inform a person's own actions a
change in belief is likely to lead to a continuing change
in a person's actions. Thus as people learn new things
about each other, and themselves, their beliefs should
change and with them should change also their actions
towards each other. This may not happen immediately as
people may have got into the habit of acting in certain
ways towards each other. They will need help in breaking
such habits.

Always it is the egalitarian agreement between members
of the group that decides what it was that was done.
Though they need the help of the group, it is the individual who has the final say in what it was that he did
experience or want and what it is that he now experiences
and wants as the result of the adequate description of
action. What he experienced in the past cannot be changed
but his present experience of past actions can be changed
as a result of re-characterisation. The special responsibility of the caseworker is to arrange meetings of people
such that action, experience and belief can be adequately
characterised. He has a further responsibility for
showing the family how to carry on this activity so that
they can cope with their personal relations more adequately in the future; so that they can do what counts as the
same thing to them, in what counts as the same situation.
The caseworker is engaged in an exercise of informal
education. Part of this work is moral, as we have seen,
for adequate and accurate description depends on honesty
in those involved. The social worker is thus committed to
encouraging this basic moral value in families.

In arranging situations in which description can take
place the caseworker obviously at least hopes that people
will be able to agree on mutually understood characterisation of action and experience (also one that he can
understand as well as the others concerned). This description is more than just a form of words for it has been
argued that it is the means by which we understand not
only ourselves but also the means by which people understand us. Our identity as persons is tied up with the
descriptions of action and experience as well. The
implication in this is that in agreeing to, and under-

standing, a description we understand each other's action
and experience. To what extent is this possible? Laing
writes (1967, p.16), 'I cannot experience your experience.
You cannot experience my experience. We are both
invisible men. All men are invisible to one another....'
This would appear to be true. As finite bodies we cannot
experience numerically the same things as another finite
body occupying a different position in time and space.
However, it must be possible to enter into the experience
of others to a greater or lesser extent. It is necessary
to return to the importance of language. 'All men are
invisible to each other', writes Laing. He should have
added that if they are, each person is invisible to himself also. We understand ourselves - become visible to
ourselves, in a common medium. We understand ourselves in
terms by which other people understand themselves, and in
terms by which we understand other people and by which
they understand us. In addition it was argued that
language itself demands a mutually understood and followed
practice. Men would be invisible to each other only if a
single use of language were possible. They are visible to
each other and to themselves because they understand themselves and each other in terms of a common system of
meaning. Thus it must be possible to enter into the
experience of others to the extent that we and they understand the language used to describe it.
    So from the caseworker's point of view it is possible
to enter into the client's experience. A further matter
is the client's linguistic ability. For someone unsophi-
sticated in the elaborated code the description of
individual experience may be difficult. In this case the
experience is relatively inaccessible to the caseworker;
more important though, it is also inaccessible to the
client. It is possible that the linguistic inability may
be compensated by a non-verbal expressiveness in gesture
and other somatic symbolism such as crying and groaning,
which conveys the present experience and feeling about
what is being discussed. It conveys it both to the client
and the caseworker. The caseworker thus has the choice of
helping the client to communicate his experience in the
ways that come easiest to him or of teaching him new ways,
e.g. assisting him to a mastery of the elaborated code.
    The caseworker's task in the description of action and
feeling and the possibility of his entering into the
experience of the client has been outlined. However, he
and the client cannot ignore the physical facts of the
situation. A description of such facts is a less complex
matter than the description of action or experience
because the language here consists of a straightforward

word/object relationship to reality. What is being
described is a public material object or recurring
process. It is here that we come on an important aspect
of the caseworker's specialisation. As a result of his
education and training he may know things about the
client's situation of which the client is unaware. He may
know the implications and prognosis of the client's
medical or psychiatric condition for instance or, if the
client is not the patient, of the client's relative's
condition. He may know more about the social and institutional structure of society and thus be able to describe
its effect on the client's situation and the uses he could
make of it. The important thing is that the caseworker
does not use this specialist knowledge to diagnose the
client's situation but adds it to the material out of
which the client builds his final description. The knowledge is made subject to the logic of personal language
and the structure of personal relations.

The facts, the description of action and experience,
constitute a description of a facet of the client's
reality. As Peter Winch said, the concepts we have frame
what counts as reality for us. Thus the description is
the client's reality. This description relates that
aspect of reality being described to the present situation,
giving it meaning and significance in relation to the
client's immediate present. This is inevitably so, for
the description is of reality as it appears at a specific
place and time. It is reality as it appears to the client
in his unique situation, not something apart from him as a
person. In addition it is a personal description and will
therefore describe not only what he thought, felt, and
did, then, but what he feels and thinks about it now. An
adequate description will include both the client's
present thoughts and also his present feelings about the
matter being described.

Raymond Williams argued that description was a creative
act. We can now see that this is so in three ways. First,
the description of action and experience realises the
nature of that action and experience for the client, so
creating an aspect of his identity. Second, the total
description, including the facts, events and processes,
remakes an aspect of the client's reality. Third, the
total description includes the significance of that
situation for the present. It is a description of the
present reality of the client as well as of a past
situation. It is a reorganisation of his present world.
In doing this the client also reorganises his experience
of the world, for as Peter Winch argued, we experience, as
well as perceive, the world in terms of the concepts we
have of it.

In the foregoing it is possible to see a specialist role for the caseworker. He is able to contribute to the modification of the client's perception and experience of the world by contributing specialist material to the description. He thus has an educational role once more.

We should remember in all this that description of experience cannot be exhaustive. We have seen above that Wittgenstein was not denying the validity of inner experience, only denying that words describing it are used in a certain way like words describing natural objects. This means that there may be something left over unrealised in the description. Other aspects of experience may be only partially realised: the client may be aware of what he may describe as 'a weight of frustration'. Such unrealised or partially realised experience may continue to influence the client and affect the decisions he makes and the character of the actions he chooses. In formulating his wants (the objectives of his actions) this semi-inchoate feeling will be as important as that which is realised, but others will be unaware of it. They may wonder that he wants something that seems at variance with what he has described. In some people who make little attempt to describe, or otherwise realise, their emotions and experience, wants and actions will be formulated and chosen in relation to such unformulated material. They may then seem largely inexplicable to other people including the caseworker.

As a footnote we should remind ourselves that the description of emotion, action and significance described above is a formal replacement of the confirmation (or correction) of everyday actions that normally takes place in the course of conversation and discussion and ordinary living. Formal description becomes necessary when this confirmation or correction has gone awry and, as in the cases Laing describes, people see each other as doing very different sorts of things. Eventually they see whole situations differently. This is not to say that formal description never takes place in the course of ordinary life. In every family people are from time to time concerned about what is going on between them and try to get to the bottom of it by describing their intentions, reasons and objectives. It is when this rarely or never happens in a family or when it is done inadequately that the situations described by Laing and Esterson develop. It is in these situations that casework help can be beneficial.

THE WORK OF R. D. LAING AND DESCRIPTION

R. D. Laing and others have laid enormous emphasis on
experience and its relation to behaviour (1967, ch.1).   He
does not, however, examine the concept of experience
itself.   This appears to lead to some mis-emphasis and
unnecessary pessimism.   A great deal of what has been said
above relates to the construction of experience and
indicates how experience can be made more or less meaningful through description and more or less adequate through
proper description.   The activity of description is thus a
vital one for a person's sense of identity.   Laing also
describes the actions that people perform on each other's
experience: mechanisms or methods by which society or
individuals try to alter a person's experience so that it
becomes what they think it should be.   Laing (1969, p.2)
writes: 'Let us call the experiential structure A, and
the public event B.   It sometimes happens that the product
of A and B, in a marriage ceremony, is a marriage.... I
suspect that one of the functions of rituals is to pin A
on to B at certain critical moments in the life of a
social group....'   The mechanisms which are used in
dealing with experience, usually to normalise it, are, he
writes, what the psychoanalysts call defence mechanisms.
Experiences are 'denied', or 'projected' on to others and
condemned, 'displaced' from a person with whom they are
unacceptable on to one with whom they are acceptable.
These mechanisms can be put together as 'operations' which
have their own rules.   He writes (1969, p.32):
   The operations I described are usually not experienced
   at all.   Yet with their help most of us flesh out a
   world of sorts.   With great labour, a wish is
      (i)   denied
     (ii)   replaced by a fear that generates a nightmare
             that is
    (iii)   denied, and on which a
     (iv)   nice face is then placed
   (denial, replacement, denial replacement) - a comparatively simple four step sequence.
      Almost any operations are sanctioned if they help to
   serve up a 'normal' product.   It is difficult to behave
   sufficiently 'normally' to get by without using such
   tricks.
   This describes a mechanism that a person operates on
his own experience in order to make it what other people
want it to be.   The mechanisms are used on the experience
of others too, when it disturbs us too much.   He writes
(1967, p.31):

These 'defences' are action on oneself. But 'defences'
are not only intrapersonal, they are transpersonal. I
act not only on myself, I can act upon you. And you
act not only on yourself, you act upon me ... in each
case on experience. If Jack succeeds in forgetting
something, this is of little use if Jill continues to
remind him of it. He must induce her not to do so. The
safest way would not be just to make her keep quiet
about it, but to induce her to forget it also. Jack
may act upon Jill in many ways. He may make her feel
guilty for keeping on 'bringing it up'. He may invalidate her experience. This can be done more or less
radically. He can indicate merely that it is unimpor-
tant or trivial, whereas it is important and significant to her. Going further, he can shift the modality
of her experience from memory to imagination: 'It's
all in your imagination.' Further still, he can
invalidate the content. 'It never happened that way.'
Finally, he can invalidate not only the significance,
modality and content, but her very capacity to remember
at all, and make her feel guilty for doing so into the
bargain.

These 'mechanisms' and 'operations' he defines as being
transpersonal yet impersonal processes of which a person
can become aware. In 'Knots' (1970) he gives examples of
conversations and descriptions underlying which some of
these mechanisms can be said to be at work. These mechanisms do not seem to be verbal performances of the sort
that Austin described, yet they appear to have features in
common with actions. In the first place they can be
brought to awareness so that people can understand what
they are 'doing'. They appear to be actions at the level
of 'just being and doing'. Second, that they are taking
place would seem to depend on agreement between the agent,
the person acted upon, and observer(s). What is agreed
seems to be the perlocutionary character of the action.
Laing (1967, p.29) writes: 'Personal action can either
open out possibilities of enriched experience or it can
shut off possibilities. Personal action is either pre-
dominantly validating, confirming, encouraging, supportive,
enhancing, or it is invalidating, disconfirming, dis-
couraging, undermining and constricting. It can be
creative or destructive ' If Jack says to Jill, 'You are
imagining it', he has performed a perfectly correct
locutionary act. In performing it he has uttered what is
called a statement (the illocutionary character). The
perlocutionary effect will depend on the situation existing between Jill and Jack and what she sees him as doing.
This will depend on how she sees the situation as a whole

and how she sees his act within this. She understands him within the social context that she understands to exist between and around them. Thus the action could be creative or destructive. Which it is would depend on the agreement they came to (egalitarian, unforced). They would have to take into account each other's reasons for acting and what it was they wanted and were trying to achieve by acting in the way that they were. Honesty and sincerity would be essential in this characterisation. Laing tries to illustrate how people can corrupt each other's experience. He assumes that there is something called experience which everybody has. It has been argued here that something exists before it is described but that what it is cannot be known until it has been put into meaningful form. So the primary way of debasing another person would be to deprive him of the opportunity of adequately characterising the actions he performs and which are performed towards him. This would prevent him ever achieving an adequate realisation of his experience. If and after his experience has been more or less adequately realised, operations and mechanisms such as Laing described can be used on people's own and others' experience. It seems that these mechanisms are actions that people perform at the habitual level and which are often inadequately characterised. What sort of actions they are and the experience of them that people have depends on their being adequately characterised.

Characterisation of these 'mechanisms' makes great demands on the integrity of the individual concerned. If it is suggested that he is 'denying' something in what he is doing, in order to examine this he is forced to face up to something that may be extremely unpleasant or difficult. He may have to agree that in saying what he did he was denying or avoiding discussion of this other matter. On the other hand he may say that he was denying nothing as no such matter exists or that it was not relevant to what he was trying to do on this occasion. Others may still disagree with him, pointing out that such another matter does exist or that it is affecting him in ways that he does not recognise. What they are trying to do is to get him to accept this other matter as existing and in need of description or to accept that it is of more importance in characterising what he is doing than he can see. In this situation he can indulge in Spiegel's 'masking' activi-ties. He means such actions as pretending, deceiving, avoiding, lying, etc. All are actions designed to avoid telling or facing up to the truth, or possibilities of learning the truth. They too should be described.

There are thus several factors involved here. There is

the characterisation of action;   there is characterisation
of the situation, for in suggesting that there are factors
in the situation that the person is ignoring, or failing
to see as existing, it is being suggested that the
situation is other than as he sees it; then there is the
characterisation of the 'masking' action that a person
takes.

The characterisation of these factors is a delicate
business calling for considerable trust and skill amongst
family members. The contribution of the caseworker is in
showing them how to do it - what is required for the
adequate characterisation of action and experience. Hopefully the family will learn how to do it without his
presence. There is also the trust that should exist
between the caseworker and family members on which depends
the characterisation of their relationship to him and on
the basis of which they can begin to characterise their
relationships with each other. At the beginning they
should be able to rely on him to show them what they need
to do and help them to do it rather than get involved in
disputation and recrimination (neither of which things is
description). In this situation it is obviously important
that the caseworker should be able to clarify that what he
is doing is helpful and creative and not undermining and
destructive.

This sort of work is not diagnostic or concerned with
the adjustment of systems. It invokes the creative
capacity of clients. People are involved in generating
sentences to describe each other's and their own actions,
to realise their own experience. It is a creative exercise in the sense that Chomsky uses the word. Even where
their beliefs about each other are concerned they are
asked to generate new sentences to express the changes in
their beliefs.

The moral aspect of the work arrives as people begin to
assess what they have been doing to each other (without
perhaps realising it) and what they should be doing in
order to give each other an adequate personal environment.
They are concerned with each other's claim for differential treatment. At the root of each and every claim is an
understanding of what a person requires in order to
enhance his experience as a person. So the caseworker and
the family are concerned with each other not as entities
in a psychological theory but as people who in their
actions provide an environment on which others are dependent for the quality of their own experience as persons.
The caseworker is concerned not with the adjustment of
systems but with helping people to create a better environment for each other and in family casework it is the

interpersonal environment that is at the centre of
attention. He is concerned with what people can do for
and with each other.

5   Casework treatment or personal planning?

In the last chapter it was argued that description should
replace diagnosis in the practice of social work. The
result of this is to give the client responsibility for
characterising his actions, emotions and experience in the
context of the problem situation that concerns him. Under
the guidance of the social worker he learns how to do this
both adequately and accurately. The client is helped with
his problem in such a way that he also learns how to
enhance his identity as a person. What should be apparent
by now is that the social caseworker's claim to treat
people as people is contradicted in the conventional
approach by the methods used (diagnosis rather than description) and the objectives set ('mentally healthy
functioning' rather than self-realisation). What has been
suggested so far is that description should replace
diagnosis. In this chapter I hope to show how a sequence
of rational planning and moral discussion should replace
procedures designed to modify behaviour and bring about an
'adjustment of systems'.

Amongst casework writers it is customary to divide
casework problems into two sorts: those which are material
or practical with emotional and interpersonal concomitants
and those where the problem lies in the client's own
social functioning (e.g. Mayer and Timms, 1970; Hollis,
1964; Perlman', 1957). While diagnosis is discussed as a
method of social casework it is not usually included in
discussions of casework treatment. Treatment is usually
considered under two headings: procedures and goals. Goals
are frequently divided into long-term ones and immediate
ones. Client self-determination is recognised by acknow-
ledging that the client may accept or reject the treatment
offered him (e.g. Hollis, 1964, pp.204, 207-9; Smalley,
1967, pp.151-2, 167-8; Perlman, 1957, pp.125, 200-2). The
last named writers use a 'purposive' model of man and see

casework as the process that 'engages' a person in working
on his problem alongside the caseworker who, if necessary,
removes emotional 'blocks' to this activity. The long-
term goal of treatment is to narrow the gap between the
initial situation and what the caseworker perceives as
'healthy' social functioning. Short-term goals are steps
along this road.

One of the things that is lacking in all these
approaches, and which is yet said to be a principle of
fundamental importance, is an adequate understanding of
self-determination or the 'purposive'. The only real
decision that the client is offered by all 'schools' is
that of accepting or rejecting any treatment offered. Well
may Bernece Simon write (Roberts and Nee, 1970, p.365) of
the need to 'rescue the elusive doctrine of individual
self-determination from its limbo between philosophy and
psychology to take its place in the real world of principles of operation in social casework and, indeed, in
social work'. One of the things that has prevented this
is the way socio-behavioural knowledge is related to
practice: the client is constituted an aspect of the casework problem as described by the theory concerned. He is
subject to modification by the sort of techniques that are
applicable equally to all other aspects of the problem. He
is not recognised and treated as being a person and thus
qualitatively different. The goal of all approaches is to
improve 'personal-social' functioning. Yet all 'schools'
pay lip-service to 'client self-determination'. Confusion
as to its proper nature arises from subordinating it not
only to the casework problem but also to the casework
problem as described or diagnosed in 'socio-behavioural
theory'. This is clear from a study of the papers in
Roberts and Nee (1970) in which all theories accept a
socio-behavioural theory of man as the basis for social-
casework practice.

There would seem to be a fundamental difference in kind
between a personal approach and a conventional casework
one. This is a consequence of formulating a casework
problem in accordance with some theoretical framework. The
person at the centre of the problem (the client) becomes
simply a factor in the problem to be influenced. When
dealing with non-personal things it is reasonable to
strive after measures that are not only necessary but also
sufficient to produce their results; it is reasonable to
aim for complete predictability of results. If applied to
persons, however, this aim depreciates them; it fails to
attribute to the other person (the client) the capacity to
act and therefore always to have the possibility of pre-
empting the caseworker's measures. If the client is

treated as a person it must always be possible for him to
know what the caseworker is trying to do and take counter-
measures. In treating the client as a person this must be
allowed for, by never aiming to make casework methods both
necessary and sufficient to cause their results. What the
caseworker does must always be completed by the client;
the caseworker may do things necessary for a certain
objective to be achieved but its attainment depends on
further activity from the client. It might be argued that
this is true of all medical or psychological practice in
that what the specialist is trying to do is produce a
state in which certain activities become possible for the
client. In personal casework the position is somewhat
different. Client and caseworker are working co-
operatively as persons and equals; the actions of one are
complemented by the other throughout. In addition an
educational role is adopted by the caseworker. He is not
trying to produce an adjustment between systems but help
the client to learn what to do. He hopes that the client
will be able to do (or avoid doing) what counts as the
same thing in the future in similar situations. In a
personal approach the measures taken by the caseworker may
be necessary but they should never be sufficient to
produce the results. They must be completed by the other
person - the client.

THE FRAMEWORK OF A PERSONAL METHOD OF SOCIAL WORK

The substitution of description for diagnosis leads to the
client working on his own problem using his own creative
capacities as he formulates his description. The social
caseworker's role consists of trying to provide the social
situations in which adequate description can take place
and in guiding the client through the descriptive process
so that an accurate description emerges.
     In a personal approach the client must be treated as a
being capable of rational thought and action. Indeed, the
long-term goal of the personal approach is to foster the
enrichment of personal identity by encouraging the most
rational approach to personal problems. We have seen how
this is done in description; we must now see how it can be
achieved at what the conventional theories call the treatment stage.
     Of major importance in the personal approach is the
fact that a rational approach to the problem described
offers a link between society and the individual, so overcoming a basic dichotomy in social work (see chapter 3).
In chapter 2 we showed that our existence as persons

depended on there being others (society) who could join us in rule-following action. We then saw that specific actions can in principle only be characterised through communication - with the help of others. As our indivi- duality consists of our biography as agents and the recipients of experience, our character as persons depends on others whose co-operation, in principle, is needed for the characterisation of our actions and experience. In chapter 2 we also argued that after an act had been characterised a further agreement was necessary concerning its appropriateness. With treatment we become concerned with appropriateness: what a person does to solve his problem should be appropriate. What are the criteria of appropriateness? As an action is by definition performed for reasons, then the level of rationality (by Milne's scale) becomes a measure of its appropriateness. Achieving a rational solution to a problem affects the identity of the person concerned. If his character as a person is made up, in large part, of his biography as an agent, then the level of rationality at which he conducts himself will affect his character as a person. Milne's scale of rationality necessarily involves morality and a critical stance towards society. So in a personal approach, the concern with personal identity leads logically to a concern with society. In considering what to do in the face of a personal problem a person is led logically to assess alternative courses of action, not only for their efficiency in solving the situation but also for their implications for others (social justice). The scale also provides criteria deriving from the principles on which a society fit for personal life would be based. So a personal approach involves no dichotomy between the individual and society. People are seen as living and acting within society and therefore always involved with it. An assessment of the appropriateness of an action in response to a situation must logically therefore include a socio-moral dimension.

THE DISSOLUTION OF PROBLEMS

There is one way in which description, if carried out adequately and accurately, may itself solve - or dissolve - problems.   This is what might be called the dissolution of problems.
  What is described is a personal problem. It is the caseworker's task to help the client to describe a situation which is preventing him doing what he wants to do, or which confuses him to the extent that he does not

know what to do. It is possible that an adequate and
accurate description may make the problem disappear.
Though it may happen rarely this sort of solution implies
that the problem lies in the client's appreciation, and
therefore description, of the situation. It is here that
the caseworker's specialist knowledge is important.

I shall examine this in terms of the interpersonal/
emotional and material/practical division of problems
mentioned at the beginning of this chapter. Let us return
to Mrs A of Sainsbury's case history. It seems clear that
she is so confused by her situation that she does not know
what to do. An adequate and accurate description of her
situation will involve Mrs A working on her own to characterise what she was trying to do and Mrs A working with
others to characterise what she has actually done. Having
described what she was trying to do and what she has done
it may be quite clear to Mrs A what she wants to do now
and how to do it. It may become clear to her that what
she wants (and was trying to achieve all along) is separation from her husband and custody of, or access to, the
children. In this case, description resolves Mrs A's
confusion and she achieves clarity as to her long-term
goal. Put in touch with a solicitor, she can proceed
towards it. What has happened is that through characterising what she was trying to do and what she actually did,
Mrs A clarifies what she wants to do now - that is, what
she has been trying to do all along. Description
dissolves the confusion that was the problem when she came
to the social worker.

On the other hand, Mrs A may be convinced that her
husband's moods and bad temper make it impossible for her
to live at home with the family as she would like to do.
His accusations about 'bad mothering' lead her to believe
that all he wants is for her to leave the house. She
believes that the arrival of her mother-in-law is an
attempt on his part to replace her. Description may
dissolve the problem by showing her that she had 'got it
all wrong'. When Mrs A is engaged with her husband and
mother-in-law in describing the situation she may find
that her previous description was both inadequate, because
she had never sat down with her husband to describe her
actions or his feelings, and also inaccurate because her
understanding of the situation mis-stated his emotions,
his and her actions, and his and her desires. An adequate
and accurate description shows her that the situation is
other than she thought. She finds that her husband is
bad-tempered and moody because he is aware of his loathing
of physical contact. He has been unable to discuss this
with her because it had affected his relationship with

her - he was unable to show his affection for her physically and they had withdrawn from each other. He turned to his mother for help. Realising all this, Mrs A returns home. Her problem of the time that she arrived with the social worker is dissolved (although she now has another, perhaps). An adequate descriptive process had led to a more accurate description of the situation and dissolution of the problem.

Let us now turn to the material/practical dimension, again taking Mrs A as an example. Mrs A went for her walk and visited her friend in despair. She believed that if she left home her husband would gain possession of the house and control over the children. This is why she could not make up her mind whether she had left home or was on holiday. Her husband was bad-tempered and over-bearing, constantly complaining about her and not even hearing anything she might say. So confident was he, that she thought he must be right. Her problem is dissolved when she learns that she has rights in the house and the children, and that in going for divorce and separation not all rights and entitlements are on his side. Financial doubts are cleared up as she learns of the legal-aid scheme.

These are examples of how adequate and accurate description can dissolve problems (though maybe creating others). Some expertise is demanded of the social case-worker. First, that of knowing the form of an adequate description and the importance of it being factually accurate. Second, that of having the facts available, e.g. family law and the legal-aid scheme in the last example. Third, of being able to establish and maintain social relations with other individuals and within a group such that adequate description can take place (and not recriminations and quarrelling).

THE CASEWORK RELATIONSHIP IN PERSONAL SOCIAL WORK

In chapter 3 we saw how conventional theories of social work conceived the relationship between caseworker and client as an instrument to be used in moving the client towards 'more healthy functioning'. We argued that this devalued the client as a person by paying insufficient respect to the realisation of honesty in the relationship, on which personal identity depends. In this section we shall examine in more detail the nature of the relation-ship between social worker and client in a personal approach.

At the end of chapter 2 and in chapter 3 the quality of

a personal relationship was related to the extent to which
honesty is realised within it, enabling the participants
to characterise each other's and their own experience. The
intimacy of the relationship was also touched upon by
suggesting that an intimate personal relationship is one
in which there is a high degree of honesty and one in
which the relationship is an end in itself. This means
that many of the things the participants do will have the
objective of fostering the relationship between them. So
we can say that an intimate relationship is one which is
entered into for its own sake and with no more important
objective in view: it is one in which most of the actions
of the participants will be performed with the fostering
of this intimacy in mind; it is one in which the participants engage in a large number of interpersonal actions
towards each other - they encourage each other, cuddle and
kiss each other, become angry with each other, tease each
other, etc. While these things define the intimacy of a
relationship the social context defines whether this intimacy is realised within a fraternal, marital, or friendly,
etc., framework. We have now to see to what extent the
social caseworker/client relationship is intimate and how
it is personal.

INTIMACY OF THE SOCIAL WORKER/CLIENT RELATIONSHIP

The relationship between social worker and client is not
entered into for its own sake, so it lacks the main
distinguishing mark of an intimate personal relationship.
The relationship is entered into with objectives in view.
The objectives of the relationship affect its intimacy but
this does not mean that the participants are dishonest.
People can control the degree to which a relationship
becomes intimate without being dishonest or impersonal. In
any relationship that is entered into with objectives in
view, e.g. to play football; to climb a mountain; to teach
people, etc., the objective defines, roughly, the area in
which honesty is necessary - necessary for co-operation in
achieving the objective. The participants quite correctly
refrain from extending the area open to honesty beyond
what is necessary to achieve the objective.
     The objectives affect the intimacy of the relationship
in a second way. In an intimate relationship, people will
engage in co-operative activity in order to foster the
relationship as much as to achieve the objective itself.
In practical co-operation the attainment of the objective
is the main end. So the relationship between client and
worker when the objective is a practical one, e.g. to get

a landlord to carry out contractual repairs on a dwelling,
is subject to the requirements - and those alone - of any
practical co-operative endeavour. There should be sufficient honesty between people as to their ends and means to
allow them to work efficiently together.

Objectives affect the intimacy of the relationship in a
third way. Interpersonal actions are not performed for
their own sake but to facilitate the achievement of the
objective. In an intimate relationship - entered into for
its own sake - interpersonal activity is an end in itself;
in a relationship with practical objectives there is
encouragement, assistance, advice, etc., but these are
subsidiary to the main objective. They do, however,
enable a certain sort of intimacy to develop - that of
comrades in arms - with mutual rejoicing at success, great
or small, commiseration in defeat, and humour as appropriate. This type of intimacy obviously develops between
worker and client in practical social work.

If a problem is an interpersonal one, or has interpersonal dimensions, as with Mrs A, the social worker is
likely to be involved with the client(s) more intimately.
While the social worker himself is not involved in an
intimate personal relationship with the client (e.g. Mrs
A), he is privy to what is intimate in her and her
family's life. He is privy to what is usually open only
to those who are in intimate relationship; that is, the
characterisation of intimate interpersonal actions and
activity engaged in to foster intimacy. It may be that
this characterisation has been inadequate for one reason
or another; that is why the social worker is concerned
with it. It is incumbent upon him, therefore, to conduct
himself with the honesty and trustworthiness that that
level of intimacy requires.

In some cases, however, it may be the actual relationship with the caseworker itself that helps the client. In
a personal approach, this is not the result of any
relationship therapy. Rather it is the result of a
genuine human sympathy and understanding. The case described by Mary Richardson in chapter 1 is an example of
this. Values were realised in the relationship she
describes, the experience of which slowly enabled the
mother concerned to take her rightful place in the world
again. It was the experience and what she made of it that
helped her. A similar case is described by Miss M. L.
Sheppard (BJPSW, vol.7, no.1,1963), where a personal
relationship develops between the social worker and the
client. In Miss Richardson's case the bond of sympathy
was founded on the social worker's personal response to
the poverty and degradation of the mother concerned. In

Miss Sheppard's case, the response was personal, but involved a highly sophisticated understanding and interpretation of the experience of grief and persecutory delusions in old age. Miss Sheppard's understanding enabled her to make personal contact with the old lady concerned. Both examples are intimate in the sense that the caseworker enjoys the relationship to a very large extent for its own sake (which is what helps the client).

The general objectives of personal social casework are not such that in subscribing to them the caseworker undermines the relationship with the client. They are to help the client solve his problem in such a way as to enhance his identity as a person, and in so doing to enable him to learn how to conduct life in such a way as to enrich his identity as a person. Because the relationship is thus educational rather than therapeutic it is not used as an instrument to change the client's social or psychological functioning.

While these objectives affect the intimacy of the relationship, they should not affect its personal nature. This is because the objective(s) are mutually agreed. It is the pursuit of private objectives, in which one person in the relationship uses the other in achieving his own undisclosed ends, that undermines the possibility of that honesty being realised on which the establishment of personal identity depends. In avoiding one person's private objectives having this effect, the establishment of common aims is an important step. If both client and worker know what they are trying to do and why, neither need suspect the other quite so readily of pursuing private objectives: reasons and actions can be read off on each side as leading to this common aim.

Within these limitations, however, the relationship between the client and caseworker in a personal approach must obviously be personal. If one of the aims is to enable the client to strengthen his identity as a person then the relationship with the caseworker should exemplify the sort of relationship in which people can realise themselves. So description replaces diagnosis. The client is treated as someone who can act on his own behalf in describing his problem. Nor is the relationship used as an instrument of therapy. This means that the relationship between client and caseworker must have all the characteristics of a good personal relationship. It must be open and honest so that the actions each performs towards the other can be adequately described and characterised. This need not be done formally. The very reaction of each to the other will convey what action each has seen the other perform. In discussing how to meet a certain situation, the way the client takes up what the caseworker says will indicate whether he understands the caseworker to have suggested something, to have given advice, or to be persuading him to do something. No more than this may be necessary in the way of confirmation and correction of what is going on between client and caseworker as they discuss what to do, but it is important that each should be able to take up more directly what the other is doing in the relationship, especially if it makes him feel uncomfortable or annoyed (thus frustrating cooperation).

If personal identity is the key concept in social casework, it is of great importance to enable the client to realise himself as a person in relation to the caseworker. If this is to be achieved the caseworker must be open with his intellectual and emotional responses to the client's actions (otherwise the actions would not be adequately characterised). So treating the client as a person entails the caseworker responding as a person himself within the limitations described above and those imposed by the client.

This brings us to the egalitarian nature of a personal relationship. The tacit confirmation and correction that people offer each other in the course of conversation and practical action is usually unforced. It is when relationships themselves are the subject of study that confusion can arise. The relationship between client and worker can become an example to the client and his group so it is important that what is being done in that relationship should be clear, as an example. When the relationship between client and worker is itself in the centre of attention, it becomes possible for the caseworker to use his status as a professional to force the client to agree to his understanding: 'I was not persuading you: I was only making a suggestion.' If the caseworker does this, then a fatal ambiguity is introduced into the relationship. Because the caseworker insists on his interpretation, and the client knows he is insisting, what was actually done is never mutually characterised and the experience based on it may be equally ambiguous. This is avoided to some extent if each is prepared to examine the situation and set about characterising the actions and experience involved in a logically adequate way so that an accurate description emerges. Accuracy cannot be achieved, however, if one person uses his position to force or otherwise impose his opinion on the other. To refuse to accept that one has not succeeded in doing what one was trying to do, to withhold one's emotional response because of one's status, both affect the characterisation of

action and thus the understanding that the client and
caseworker have of each other as persons. For the purpose
of defining action or experience it is essential that
people meet simply as people. Whatever position they may
hold, that position does not justify one person preferring
his opinion to that of others when characterising action
or experience. There must be an egalitarian social agreement or tacit understanding as to what action has been
performed. The characterisation, if it is to be accurate,
must be between persons simply as persons. It may be very
difficult, if not impossible, for the social worker to
achieve this in the one-to-one situation, because of the
status he holds, vis-à-vis the client, in wider society.
But in a group, clients appear to be more ready to
challenge her (Sinfield, 1969).

Another matter affecting the relationship between
client and social caseworker concerns the nature of the
society in which they live. Plant, as we saw, raised the
question of the mode of participation in society, suggesting that this would vary with the character of society.
In the rational model adopted here, the social worker, as
a person, will be concerned about the nature of his
society and will himself have adopted ways of living in
it. This is bound to affect the way he relates to his
client. Both of them are people before they are occupiers
of the roles they have as client and social caseworker.
The nature of the society that makes the roles available
is bound to affect the way in which people act in the
roles. The first point that I wish to make, therefore, is
that in a personal approach to social work it is not
possible to discuss the client/social caseworker relationship in isolation from wider moral and social issues. If
the relationship is not being considered as an instrument
of therapy with which a caseworker is doing something to a
client, but as a meeting between two persons, then as
persons each will have rational beliefs and values affecting their participation in society and, therefore, their
relationship with each other.

We have shown that Milne's scale of rationality includes a perspective from which societies can be assessed
as offering conditions conducive to personal life. Milne
maintains that only a small number in any society are
likely to reach this level of rationality (critical
humanism) in a world in which no society has achieved the
position of making life at this level of rationality open
to all. However, we argued in chapter 3 that being a
person is, has been, and will continue to be, something
that can be learned. In a personal approach to social
work it is the focus of social-work activity. Therefore,

social workers should be trained in it, and by virtue of
their training be able to work and live at that level of
rationality called by Milne critical humanism. They will
be amongst the small number in any society he postulates
as being able to work at this level of rationality.

Although the caseworker may learn to act at this level
as part of his education and training as a social worker,
it is obviously learning that is not role-related but
intrinsic to his life as a person. He carries into the
client's situation the perceptions of someone living at a
high rational level (hopefully that of critical humanism).
This, as we have seen, carries with it criteria of social
justice and a critical stance on society. One possibility
that could affect the relationship between client and
caseworker is that the client might not perceive his
situation in the way that the caseworker does. On the
other hand, the caseworker, as a professional (or semi-
professional) with a recognised and well-rewarded position
in society, may be unaware of the way in which society
impinges on the lives of some of his fellows. The client
may therefore have much to teach the caseworker. It is
vital that the caseworker should be open to learn from the
client as suggested by Paulo Freire (1972). What is
important in either of these situations is that both
client and caseworker should respond as persons. In the
second of the above possibilities it is vital to a
personal approach that the caseworker should respond as
someone thinking and acting at the level Milne describes
as critical humanism. This involves being prepared to act
as indicated by considerations of social justice, but not
only this - he should also examine the client's situation
and life history to see to what extent possibilities of
self-realising activity have been open to him. If they
have not been, and are not, he should assess whether
society had and has the means and understanding to make
them available (the scientific knowledge marshalled into
rational argument). If the means and understanding are
both available in society, it is necessary to understand
further why that society does not do what it is possible
for it to do in making a full personal life available to
all its members equally, and take action as a result of
that knowledge. In the personal approach, therefore, the
caseworker is likely to be committed to a position of
solidarity with his client(s) to redress social injustice
(even if it affects the caseworker's well-being) and to
create a society more conducive to personal life (responsive to rational argument; providing, through educational,
artistic and other facilities, opportunities for self-
realisation equally to all its members, etc.).

The first possibility involves the caseworker in trying to broaden the client's rational perspective, to help him to see the issues of social justice that may be involved, and further to help him to see the rational and moral importance of trying to ensure that people in his situation have better opportunities in future. Ideally this should involve, for example, not simply solving the client's request for clothes for her single-parent children by obtaining them from the WRVS or by means of an exceptional needs grant from the SBC, but by opening her eyes to the situation of people like her in society. This is not, as a current conventional wisdom would have it, to use the client to further the caseworker's political views, but to attempt to raise the rational level of the client's thought and action according to standards to which all citizens should be committed as persons.

In a society attempting to realise the standards of critical humanism, it should be possible for a social caseworker to work in solidarity with the client, for by so doing he will be contributing to the creation of a more socially just society and one in which opportunities of self-realisation are more widely and equally available. Where and when such solidarity is prohibited as a way of working, the social caseworker surely has a responsibility, as a person, to point out that his role as a professional is being used by society to prevent him from doing what is morally incumbent on him as a person.

A real problem arises when the client cannot accept the social worker's viewpoint, when for instance he will not complain about the conduct of an SBC visiting officer following an application for an exceptional needs grant. The client may not want to cause trouble; the social worker may want to rectify abuse. If the client sees the visiting officer as harassed, underpaid or overworked and is anxious lest he should make trouble for someone as underprivileged as himself, then maybe he has a point. A way around the situation for the social worker might be to introduce the client to others who had suffered similarly and suggest that together they might devise a scheme of action, not against an individual officer but against the organisation of the service. In personal social work this would be seen not as a social worker using clients to further his political ends but as part of the educational task of enabling them to act at a higher rational level by taking action in line with a certain critique of their society as a society fit for persons.

So the long-term educational aims of personal social work should enable the social caseworker to get over any impasse he may get into with a particular client. There

are (informal educational) methods he can use to put the
client in a position at least to understand a wider perspective. If the particular client does not want to proceed there may be others in the group with whom the social
worker can continue. The theory of personal social work
allows room for the social worker to pursue the rational
perspectives adopted personally in the course of his
training.

What we see from this is that the traditional divisions
of social work (casework, group work and community work)
do not pertain in personal social work. The social worker
should be able to work with individuals, groups or collec-
tives, and in communities. The division of social work
into specialist methods almost prevents this from happening.

In considering the relationship between client and
caseworker, it should be remembered that they get to know
each other as persons and this as McMurray says (1961) is
different from knowing someone in terms of their psychology or sociology. Each person knows how much he can
trust the other; each person knows the other as an agent;
each person knows the other in relation to himself as a
person - what he feels and thinks about him, what he does
towards him. Generally, the relationship between client
and caseworker is the same as that between any two people
co-operating together. It demands that they treat each
other as persons and realise sufficient honesty and trust
between them to be able to co-operate on the job in hand
and that each is able to respond as a rational and moral
being to the client's situation.

MORAL IMPLICATIONS OF A PERSONAL APPROACH

It is by now clear that the caseworker is not involved in
a technical exercise designed to change either the
client's behaviour or his immediate social environment
with the aim of producing an 'adjustment' of the client-
in-situation. Nor is the caseworker engaged in an
exercise to bring the client up to some professional
standard of mental health. Instead, the central concept
underlying his work is that of personal identity. This
does not mean that the limit of the caseworker's horizon
is individual behaviour. Because personal existence
depends on the existence of a society of similar others,
and because the quality of that existence depends on the
character of that society, both in a wide sense and as it
impinges on the person, in being concerned about the
individual the caseworker must be concerned about society.

What remains to be said is that these methods depend on the realisation of certain fundamental values in personal relationships: honesty of response and sincerity of action. Without a general tacit recognition of the importance of these values in society as a whole and their realisation in personal relations at least to a minimum extent, the everyday tacit confirmation and correction of action and experience people offer each other would fall apart. In description, action and experience could not be adequately characterised. If he is to treat people as people the caseworker should use methods that involve his clients as persons. Description and planning are methods that do this. As delineated above they are simple formalisations of what goes on hour by hour in daily living. What is important, however, is that they depend on honesty and sincerity being realised between people. This is as true of social-casework relationships as of any other relationships between people. So, the methods the caseworker uses and encourages his clients to use, in tackling the problems they bring to him, are methods that depend on certain fundamental values. This means that the caseworker is committed to supporting and fostering these values, whether the client's problem is a practical one or one involving relationships and emotions.

Another way of putting this is in terms of positive and negative freedom. Personal relationships require more than freedom from restraint and interference; i.e. more than negative freedom. If a person acts, he cannot know what act he has performed, or whether he has succeeded in doing what he was trying to do, unless he receives a tacit confirmatory or corrective response from the other. He requires more of the other than simply to be left alone, to be free from constraint or interference. A positive decision is at some time required of the other person to act in such a way as to make it clear what he sees the agent as doing. Of course a great deal of this confirmation and correction is habitual. It happens all the time: whenever people talk to each other they confirm that they are using language correctly however much they may disagree over what is said; when one person starts washing up another takes up the drying cloth, etc., so confirming the first person as performing the action of washing-up. However, description shows how positive, on occasion, must be the effort of people to provide a response for each other on which the existence and quality of personal life depends. This is to say that personal identity depends on a positive notion of freedom in that any individual's personal identity depends on being given a certain sort of response by other people. The caseworker thus encourages

people to provide an adequate personal environment for
each other - inherent in which is the realisation of
honesty and sincerity.

A further way in which the caseworker is committed to
morality appears with a consideration of what he does in
encouraging people to act rationally rather than habitually - 'blindly just being or doing'. In chapter 4 we
argued that it was rational to be moral: in taking others
into account when planning action a person supports the
social network around him, but in supporting it he is
committed to the principle of justice. So in promoting
rational action the caseworker is also committed to promoting morality and the principle of justice. It is justifiable for the caseworker to put the interests of others
and the demands of justice to his client(s).

This commitment to morality and the fundamental values
of honesty and sincerity necessarily also commits the
caseworker against those acts described by Spiegel as
'masking' (Spiegel, 1960). Such acts militate against
this honesty: lying, deceiving, prevaricating, etc.

A further factor in providing an adequate personal
environment is the response to rational argument. To
treat someone as a person is to treat him as an agent.
This means that one responds to his rational arguments by
changing one's own ways; it means also that one expects
him to try to change his ways in response to one's own
arguments. The fostering of sincere and rational discussion is another way in which the caseworker encourages the
creation of an adequate environment for personal life. It
also involves morality in that each trusts the other to
argue and respond honestly.

The case of Mrs A illustrates some of this in practice:
for her to realise what it is that she has done, an honest
response is required of, amongst others, her husband and
her mother-in-law. In doing this all concerned are providing an adequate personal environment for each other: each
should respond to the other with that honesty on which the
characterisation of all action and experience (and consequently personal identity) depends. This involves them in
being open about their reasons and objectives in doing
what they did, otherwise the situation will never be described. The caseworker, too, should be honest about his
reasons for inviting them to undertake this exercise: not
until the whole situation is properly characterised can
any plan of action be devised to meet it. The characterisation of 'masking' activities may well be important.
When deeply ingrained habitual actions are under examination, such as Mr A's loathing of physical contact with the
children, characterisation may become painful, as Raymond

Williams points out. People such as Mr A may unwittingly
resort to 'masking' actions to avoid further description.
It is here that the caseworker may be of some help by
illuminating the 'masking' exercise and so helping the
description to go forward. Another thing he can do is to
help Mr and Mrs A respond to each other's rational arguments especially where child-rearing is concerned. From
the description Sainsbury gives, it appears that they have
both retreated behind their accusations about each other:
over-protectiveness and distaste of physical contact. In
exploring these accusations rationally rather than compet-
itively, their relevance to the rearing of the children
might be clarified, and Mr and Mrs A treat each other
fully as people in the process.

So in working with problem relationships, the caseworker demands of those concerned a high degree of sincerity in describing their emotions and thoughts about each
other's actions. Only thus can the actions be properly
characterised. At the same time he is engaged in the
educational work of enabling people to provide an essential part of an adequate environment for personal life for
each other, what they must do to support and enhance each
other's identity and experience as persons. The methods
used are those which, in this and other situations, will
also develop personal identity.

It has been argued that in order to assist an individual with a problem such as Mrs A's the caseworker should
call on relevant others to assist in the description of
the situation, the emotions and actions involved, and to
engage in the planning of a course of action. This means
(hopefully) that the caseworker is frequently one of a
group of people. If his interest is focused on what
people are doing or planning to do, rather than 'bringing
about an adjustment', he cannot ignore the moral implications of what goes on. In the example of Mrs A, what
she does (and has done) will have implications for others
such as her husband, children and mother-in-law. (To
treat the situation as one in which the professional task
is to bring about 'an adjustment of systems' is to deny
the ethical significance of what is being done.) Suppose
she is discussing with the caseworker, her husband and
maybe her mother-in-law whether she should leave home. She
is asking to do something that other members of the group
do not want her to do and she may also be asking for them
to agree that she is justified in doing it. Examining
whether Mrs A is justified in leaving the family group
involves, amongst other things, examining the way the
family has treated her. The fact that she wants to leave
the family may indicate that its members have not been

providing her with an adequate personal environment.
Logically, if the family is interested in the question,
they should be prepared to examine their treatment of her
in general. Important among her reasons for wanting to
leave are disagreements about the rearing of the children.
It seems that she and Mr A have both adopted fixed
positions on this without examining their reasons further:
Mr A seems unwilling to look at his purported loathing of
physical contact and Mrs A seems unwilling to examine
closely the accusation of over-protectiveness. Each may
be avoiding further inquiry by sticking rigidly to the
accusation made about the other - a masking activity.
Their treatment of each other on this issue may be sympto-
matic of their treatment of each other in general. Their
relationship is not characterised by that honesty which we
saw was necessary to the characterisation of action and
experience, nor do they heed or respond to each other's
arguments. So Mrs A's request leads to the family group
considering the request's reasonableness in the light of
their treatment of her. They may find it a reasonable
request and be prepared to alter the way in which they
treat her in order to make it possible for her to stay.
The request should also be considered in relation to the
rearing of children. This discussion makes it clear that
moral issues in particular cases involve detailed knowledge of the facts. These include what is known about the
mother's importance to the child in its upbringing - the
effects of maternal deprivation and separation. Relevant
also will be knowledge of community attitudes to single-
parent families and divorced or separated women. The
scientific validity of this knowledge is, obviously, of
great importance.

    In this situation the family are considering the ration-
ality of various courses of action in view of the family
circumstances. They have a comprehensive description of
the family situation and Mrs A's wants. They have available, from the caseworker, various facts about child-
rearing and about prevailing attitudes, national and
local, to women who leave their families. What has to be
determined is the level of rationality at which Mrs A
would be acting should she leave home.

    In assessing the situation it is very difficult to know
what weight to put on its various aspects. How valid is
the conventional, professional wisdom on maternal separation? How is this to be compared with the effect on Mrs A
and her opportunities of self-realisation should she stay
with the family? How will family members feel if she
stays but is miserable? There is no guaranteed method of
weighing such factors against each other to produce a

correct course of action. Two things are important.
First, that family members should enter into a dialogue in
which each is prepared to try to respond, in terms of his
own conduct, to the arguments. Second, there is the
extent of circumstances Mrs A (and others) takes into
account in considering the problem. The levels on Milne's
scale are determined by the breadth of circumstances the
agent takes into account in conduct and the consideration
of conduct. If Mrs A considers only how to realise her
ambition to leave the family, she will act at the self-
regarding level with only her own well-being in mind. The
moment she begins to weigh the wishes of others against
her own and the factors mentioned in the last paragraph
she moves to the other-regarding levels of thought and
action. And when she begins to think, not in terms of
justice according to existing standards of conduct and
morality but according to what could be done to enhance
the personal life and identity of all members of the
family, whatever the conventional and accepted wisdom
might be, she moves to the level of critical humanism.

The caseworker, as one (hopefully) trained in the
methods of establishing and enhancing personal identity,
is in fact working in Mrs A's own interests in asking her
to take note of the interests of others, for this
encourages her to act more rationally; he is also justified in arranging situations in which Mrs A can enter into
dialogue with others and respond (with them) to the arguments presented. The caseworker is thus involved in a
moral exercise with the client. He asks the client to
realise in his interaction with others those values on
which personal life and society itself depend; he asks the
client to act for other-regarding as well as self-
regarding reasons; he asks the client and those close to
him to create an environment in which personal life may be
developed; he asks the client to solve problems at the
highest possible rational level.

In the planning of future action the caseworker is a
member of the client's group. His is one of the voices
that contributes to the account of what is going on between people here-and-now, and what should be done to meet
the situation confronting the client. He plays his part
in carrying out any action planned. So the rational and
moral nature of what is decided is personally important to
him.

In discussing the caseworker's relationship with the
client we noted several limitations on its intimacy. This
does not mean that the caseworker is not committed to
taking up a moral position to whatever may emerge. In the
first place he must show himself prepared to learn from

the attitudes and facts presented by the client just as he expects the client to learn from the specialist facts he presents. Second, just as he asks the client and his group to respond to rational argument, he must be prepared to respond to the arguments put to him. Third, just as he may ask the client and his group to characterise what they have done and are doing to each other, either directly or indirectly, so must he be prepared for the characteris- ation of his interaction with others with the egalitarian relations this involves. Fourth, the standards of action he is asking the client to follow should be followed by him also. If, for instance, these lead him into support- ing what may be the counter-cultural conduct of Mrs A deserting her family, he should be prepared to do so. Equally, he may, in other situations, be led into action in opposition to his employing agency (see Myra Garrett case, 'Case Con', April 1973). This course he should also be prepared to follow.

A major difficulty is the caseworker's unique member- ship of the client's (family) group. Others in the group may well have a background of common experience and shared ideas and attitudes. Full comprehension of the client's situation may be closed to the caseworker because he does not share this common background of experience. He does not share membership of this particular family over time; he does not share family members' experience of the neighbourhood and locality from the vantage point of that particular family; he may not share that family's experi- ence of occupying a certain place in the social-class structure, etc. The importance of description is obvious here: it is what makes experience factual and accessible. Sometimes the client and his group may make decisions on the basis of experience that has not been described. Such decisions are likely to be strange to the caseworker who does not take into account the large areas of experience that he does not share with the client. For example, the caseworker may be surprised by Mrs A's decision to leave the family despite all that she has heard about the likely ill-effects on the children. Such a decision may be taken on the basis of experience that has not been described and yet is overwhelming in its misery. The other side of this coin is the caseworker's own experience which he does not share with the client and/or his group. As his voice con- tributes both to the characterisation of current action and experience and the planning of future action, it is important that this voice should not be dominated by un- shared and undescribed experience and beliefs leading the caseworker to make inappropriate suggestions. So descrip- tion is as important for the caseworker as for the client.

It is important for the development of trust that differences of belief and experience (where relevant as judged by both) should be made plain to the client. There are two things that may preserve the caseworker from advising inappropriate measures. One of these is that he should remember that the least he can do is encourage the client (and his group) to adopt various rational vantage points in considering what to do. If he sticks to this he will avoid the inappropriate. The second factor is based on his remembering that the client is in a better position than he to decide questions of relevance that is, what is appropriate action. If the client has considered the situation from the standpoints suggested by Milne and has grasped all that the caseworker has to offer in the way of specialist knowledge, then it surely behoves the caseworker to accept the judgment of the client and/or his group, for they are in command of the most facts. What the caseworker should not do is to decide what is and what is not the rational and moral thing to do in the client's situation. He has no authority to say that such and such a course of action is inappropriate if he knows that that action is the result of consideration at the highest rational level. The only exceptions to this are when the proposed course of action involves violence or dishonesty, both of which, as we have seen, are destructive of society and therefore of personal identity itself.

The unique feature of the caseworker's presence in the group or with the client is that he is there to help. That he can do so cannot be assumed. Working with people as people demands that he find his place in the group on each separate occasion. It is important that he clarifies his position in the group (and at the same time claims it). To do this he will have to explain his methods: description, planning, the use of specialist knowledge, the co-operative nature of the exercise, etc. This may be done formally or it may be done tacitly or it may be done both ways, as the group moves from accepting the caseworker's suggestions and position to challenging and changing them. In the case of the A family, for instance, Mr and Mrs A may accept the value of coming together to discuss the situation with the help of the caseworker. However, if the description of their feelings and actions becomes painful they may want to question the exercise. At this point the caseworker will give a more formal explanation of what he is doing. He may also have to enter into a discussion of relevance. This may well lead to a detailed discussion of objectives. Mrs A may say that all she wants is some help in getting a lawyer and some guidance through the courts. Other members of the family may have

different ideas. The caseworker may have, too. It has
been said that one of the problems of casework is that
frequently it is not clear who the client is: the individual presenting the problem or the family. We have already explained that in order to work with the individual
person it is preferable to involve those around him in
order to secure an unambiguous sense of identity. Where
Mrs A is concerned it is necessary therefore to discuss
the whole situation with those concerned (her husband and
mother-in-law) in order to clarify what it is that she is
doing in leaving the family. In working with persons
there is no dilemma as to whether the caseworker should
work with the individual client or the whole family. In
order to work effectively with the individual those
immediately close to him must be involved. Well has
Ruddock (1969, p.109) suggested that personal identity is
the thread running through social casework.

Another major difficulty for the caseworker also arises
out of his membership of groups in society to which the
client does not belong. He may find that actions demanded
of him by the client are frowned on by those other groups
of which he is a member, most particularly the agency by
which the caseworker is employed. In thinking out such
problem situations the caseworker should adopt the standpoint of critical humanism, for he has to work out what he
should do as a person on whom different groups are making
conflicting demands. The moral demands on him as a person
are important in two ways: to him as a person, and to him
in relationship to the client, for how he conducts himself
is a model for the client. It is part of his task therefore to respond rationally and morally as a person. An
agency that interfered with this would be not only frustrating him as a person but also his professional task.
Dilemmas in this area should be shared with the client.
This would make it clear that both client and caseworker
were adopting the same position rationally and increase
the sense of solidarity between them. It is important for
the caseworker as a person and it is important vis-à-vis
the client that he should adopt the same stance as he
encourages his clients to adopt when confronting problem
situations. As a person and citizen of the same society
as the client he wants to see that society as fit a
society for personal life as possible. Any threat to the
principle of justice that like cases should be treated
alike or there be justifiable grounds for treating people
differently is a threat to him just as it is to the
client (though maybe not so immediately). He is therefore
committed as a person both rationally and morally to
procuring justice for the client even at the cost of his

own short-term security and well-being. This may not be
easy when the caseworker may be part of, or closely
related to, the social institution against which the
client has a complaint. Indeed, it may not be in his best
short-term interest to take up the cudgels on behalf of
the client. However, the caseworker can probably rely on
some sympathy from society when he is trying to achieve
justice under the law. The situation becomes more proble-
matic when injustice appears to have been caused by
deficiencies in the administration of the law, by gaps in
the law, and by legislation that seems to be at variance
with a concept of society fit for persons, i.e. unjust
law. Indeed, viewed from this standpoint, much of what
goes on under the law may appear unjust.

No clear-cut answer can be given as to what the caseworker should do in general in such situations other than
that he should consider them from the standpoint of
critical humanism and do what he can to achieve a society
fit for persons (which can be assessed by the criteria
given in chapter 2). It is incumbent upon him as a person
to do this. While society itself may fall far short of
providing, generally, an environment fit for persons, the
social caseworker (as any other person) can attempt to
realise in his personal relations the conduct and values
conducive to personal life. With this in mind the social
caseworker can discuss his problem with the client(s). In
doing so he makes clear his criticisms of society in
general and that aspect of it which is impinging on his
(personal) work with the client(s). This demonstrates
that in meeting his problems the caseworker attempts to
think and act at the same level as he encourages his
client(s) to do. And, further, this either establishes a
solidarity between them (should they have adopted a
counter-cultural position) or acts as an example. His
professional role should not prevent the caseworker from
engaging in such open discussion with the people who are
his clients, for to do so is part of his task in a
personal approach. In addition it would seem that a
society committed to providing a fit environment for
personal life should welcome criticism of the sort that
the caseworker and client may be making. If it does not
(or particular institutions do not) then both client and
caseworker have a responsibility as persons (whatever the
limitations of their roles in a deficient society) to
persevere with their criticisms and critical activities.

This does not mean that the caseworker is using the
client to further his political beliefs (as some conventional critics maintain). The caseworker may well have
political beliefs about what sort of social system is most

likely to produce a society fit for persons and the course
of action most likely to produce it. Undoubtedly the
standpoint I have described shades off imperceptibly into
politics. However, in itself it does not entail any
specific systematic political belief. It simply maintains
that any rational being must see himself as part of a
society which affects him and others through its roles and
institutions. People are political in the sense described
here (adopting a critical attitude to their society from
the standpoint of critical humanism), but not in the sense
of adopting a party-political point of view. It would,
however, seem that the political attitude here described
is a necessary preliminary to adopting a more ideological
and systematic political stance.

THE DESCRIPTION OF WANTS

We are now in a position to discuss the process of personal planning which replaces, in the personal approach,
the treatment phase in conventional theories. Before any
plan of action can be devised, however, the client must be
clear about what he wants. So we must first discuss the
description of wants. As with the description of action
and emotion, this is something that has to be done by the
client himself. What a person wants, as we saw in chapter
2, he, by definition, must try to get (or have good
reasons for not so trying). So in describing what he
wants, the client might appear to be describing the objectives for himself and the caseworker to work towards. This
is not strictly so. What a person wants, ultimately, is
to engage in some activity or partake of an experience
worth while in itself. Only the person himself – the
client – can do this. The social worker can help the
client to a situation in which he can do or experience
what he wants. So after the client has described his
wants, common objectives for the co-operation of client
and caseworker should be established. These objectives
are what would enable the client to engage in the activities and undergo the experiences desired.
    Often the description of wants and the establishment of
objectives merge into each other. What the client wants
may be something very practical such as the tenancy of a
house, or a wheelchair. Such things are wanted, not for
their own sake, but for the experiences and activities
their possession makes possible. So obvious are these
that client and worker assume them. There are, however,
occasions when what a client wants may not quite so
obviously open the door to intrinsically valuable experi-

ence and activity. For example, Mrs A may say that she
wants a divorce. Quite clearly she has a right to work
for separation from her husband. But will this give her
the opportunity for the experiences and activities that
she ultimately desires? It is clearly a delicate matter
and an action open to misinterpretation for the caseworker
to begin to explore whether divorce will give Mrs A the
opportunities that she wants, but he must surely do it. If
in fact Mrs A concludes, after detailed discussion, that
separation from her husband will not give her what she
wants, then there has been a helpful separation of objectives and ultimate desires.

Very often description of a problem situation leads
into the description of wants. For example, in trying to
describe what she was doing, Mrs A will be forced to describe what she wants. To clarify the confusion that she
was, and is, in, she will have to characterise what it is
that she ultimately wants. Here the caseworker's task is
to help her to think deeply about what she wants - the
experience of family life (with a different man or the
same one conducting himself differently) or the experiences open to an independent single woman. He also has
the task of helping her to distinguish between what she
wants and her idle wishes, day-dreams, etc.

It may be useful to characterise wants in the presence
of those likely to be affected. Mrs A, for example, may
find that what she wants changes as she notes the effect
of her description on her family. She may also decide
not to try to get what she wants because to do so would
necessitate her engaging in actions, or produce results,
that she did not want. For example, she might become
aware for the first time of the deep effect of her departure on her child.

The discussion of objectives may be straightforward and
obvious or it may call on considerable expertise from the
social worker. Where emotions and relationships are concerned it may be very difficult for the social worker to
say what measures will put, for example, Mrs A in the
position to enjoy better marital relations with her husband. He can, however, explain the importance of each of
them offering the other an environment in which personal
development can take place. He can also offer to help
them to do it.

In the discussion of the action necessary to achieve
objectives, discussion with others is a logical necessity.
What the client and caseworker propose to do is characterised in large measure by those likely to be affected.
Their perceptions and emotions are important facts that
should be incorporated in any description. Engaging them

in the discussion is necessary so that these facts can be
known. Without this knowledge the client could not
(except by chance) produce an accurate description. He
might end up by doing something quite other than what he
was trying to do. And when others know what he is trying
to do they may perceive his action differently (see
chapter 3). Accurate description of proposed action is as
important for the client's sense of identity as it is with
past or present action. The presence of others is important from a practical point of view also: their co-
operation or neutrality can be secured or plans changed to
secure it.

Very often caseworker, client and family or other support group will discuss and characterise a proposed action
but they will have to guess at the response of others –
the housing authority, the school, Social Security, grand-
parents, neighbours, etc. What they are guessing at, however, is not only people's response to a pre-defined
action, but also as to what action they will see it as
being. These others are part of the environment that
characterises the action. How the discussants guess this
will affect what it is that the client eventually does.
What will such-and-such an official or agency see the
client as doing? Will an appeal against the SBC be seen
as 'bloody-minded' or an acceptable assertion of rights?
It is here that the caseworker can be a very useful member
of a planning group, because of his personal and general
knowledge of these others. He has some understanding,
derived from his training, of possible 'role reactions'
and 'institutional points of view'. He may also know some
of the people concerned in his official capacity. He may
be able to inform these people beforehand as to the
reasons and intentions informing a proposed action. This
is not manipulation of the client; it is giving others
necessary information on which they may base their characterisation of the client's action. Such a course of
action should be agreed with the client. (In this situation, of course, the possibilities of suspicion, dupli-
city, subterfuge and misinterpretation are legion.)

In planning a course of action the caseworker may be
useful because of his special knowledge in that he can
suggest the likely unintended consequences of an action.
He can also bring out facts in the situation of which the
client may be unaware: medical, legal, psychological and
sociological facts. Such contributions may lead the
client to change his plans. He may also be able to
suggest, when it seems relevant, that a person's unrealised emotions or unrecognised beliefs are affecting the
actions he is proposing. It was mentioned above how

important such factors could be in the generation of
action. All that can be done if this is so is to return
to description and try to make meaningful what is inchoate.

In general the client will want a way of relating, with
and amongst those around him, that is different from what
pertains at present, or he may want something more concrete than this - more money, a house, a child taken into
care, a wheelchair. All these, however, he wants in order
that he may engage in activities that are at present
closed to him. Attaining what he wants will enable him to
engage in some worth-while human activity through which
some degree of self-realisation can be achieved. There
are three ways in which the caseworker (as any other
person) may help. First, through his understanding of the
concept of wanting he can help the client adequately to
state his wants. Second, he can help the client to set
objectives and plan action to achieve them. Third, he can
participate in putting the plan into action. Here his
special position as a member of the client group, but with
access to, and membership of, other groups closed to those
in the client's group, can be immensely valuable. At all
these stages the caseworker's factual knowledge is of
great value.

The objectives of the caseworker are those of the
client and his group - to solve the problem or to attain
what the client and those around him want (unless he finds
it unjust or unethical: as a person he can then refuse
help). His immediate objective is a joint one with the
client. His long-term objective is an educational one. He
hopes that the client (and his group) will learn how to
cope with their problem, and similar problems, without his
help (though it may well be that some, perhaps many, problems can only be solved with the help of someone with
access to the resources and influence available to the
caseworker). There is also a sense in which the educational aims extend into the personal sphere. By enabling the
client to grasp more adequately those actions that enhance
his sense of identity as a person (description of action,
experience and wants; engagement in action at a high
rational level), the caseworker enables the client to
achieve a greater sense of personal identity.

At this point the nature of the caseworker's involvement with the client and his group should be mentioned. It
has been said above that his relationship with the client
is a personal one; that in working with him personally the
involvement of those close to the client is necessary;
that the caseworker has a special contribution to make. In
discussing description it was emphasised that the caseworker could not contribute a great deal other than his

understanding of the logic of description. In the description of wants and the planning of future action the caseworker can take a much more positive part. But he acts as a person in egalitarian relationship with other members of the group. This is necessary if his relationship to the client and others is to remain personal. He is a member of the client's group as a person, but as a person with a potentially special contribution to make. He must, however, claim from the others the right to make this special contribution. He makes this claim through rational argument and statement of what he thinks he can contribute. Any special position he has in the group has to be 'won' in this way, it has to be granted to him by other members of the group; and it can be taken away from him if his ways are seen by the group as being unsuccessful, unwelcome or unacceptable. In the case of Mrs A, the caseworker could do much in bringing the interested people together, helping them to describe their feelings and wants, suggesting plans of action. The family would be giving the caseworker a special position in the group by allowing him to take responsibility for doing those things, but if any of them did not like what he was doing, did not like his suggestions or interpretations, they could suggest the group did otherwise. While not losing his place as a group member, the caseworker's position in it would change as others adopted what he had claimed as the special position and contribution he could make. This of course applies to all the group members in their claims for special positions on the basis of the special contributions they think themselves capable of making. Of course these claims are not made formally, as at a council meeting for instance; in making a suggestion about how to proceed, the caseworker (or anyone else) is advancing a claim at the same time. If this suggestion is adopted and seen as successful he will be listened to more readily next time, thereby gradually winning (or losing) himself a special position in the group. It is in such informal ways that people claim and are granted special positions in a group.

SOCIAL-WORK METHODS: RADICAL SOCIAL WORK

Once common objectives have been established, methods of realising them move to the centre of attention. It is in the realm of method that there have been attempts to move away from conventional social casework. This has led many workers to adopt community work as the only acceptable way of working. Believing that interpersonal and emotional problems are either the product of the client's social situation and also a problem to the institutions of society because of the client's social situation (of deprivation or relative lack of resources), such workers think the only honest way of tackling personal problems is to change society. There have, however, been attempts to develop a 'radical' social casework at which individual problems are tackled, emotional as well as practical. In this section the positions adopted by radical casework will be taken as starting-points in delineating a personal approach.

Radical casework

Nicholas Bond (1971) argues that:
   since most social workers tend to explain their
   client's behaviour in terms of individual psychology
   there is an ever-present danger that adaptive behaviour
   by the client may be misinterpreted by the caseworker
   as maladaptive and a manifestation of the client's
   inadequacy. For example, it is quite common to hear
   social workers explain many of their clients' problems
   by their 'inability to look ahead'. However, for certain large categories of clients - unsupported mothers,
   for example - not looking ahead is frequently the only
   adaptive way of coping with a situation where to look
   ahead is to look forward to a week, a month, or even a
   lifetime of suffering. In such situations, if the
   caseworker misinterprets the client's reasons for
   living from day-to-day, not only will the worker find
   it extremely difficult to induce the client to look
   ahead but, to the extent that she is successful, all
   sorts of harmful consequences for the client, ranging
   from depression to suicide, may ensue.
The alternative put forward is an understanding of the client in terms of the client's experience. This under-lines the importance of description as a method of realis-ing this experience.
   Martin Rein (1970) describes what a 'radical social caseworker' should, in general, attempt to do:
   [It] would mean not merely obtaining for clients social
   services to which they are entitled or helping them
   adjust to their environment, but also trying to deal
   with the relevant people and institutions in the
   client's environment that are contributing to their
   difficulties. That is to say, social workers must get
   the school to adjust to the needs of poor children as
   well as getting the poor children to adjust to the

demands and routines of the schools. They must force
landlords to maintain their clients' housing as well as
helping poor families to find somewhere to live.... In
short, then, a radical casework approach would mean not
merely obtaining for clients the services to which they
are entitled or helping them adapt to the expectations
of their environment, but it would also encourage the
individuals to alter their external circumstances as
well as seeking directly to change the framework of
expectation and the level of provision that are contributing to these difficulties. Social workers need to
emphasise skill in practising casework in a hostile
rather than a benign environment - casework that is
directed not so much at encouraging conformity ... but
to marshalling the resources of clients to challenge
'reality'.

In this quotation we see that 'radical casework' consists
in concentrating on the client's environment rather than
his psychology and in encouraging the client to do things
himself about that environment rather than making him
dependent on the caseworker who does it all for him
(though there may well be things that the caseworker alone
can do, or can do much more easily, because of his
position in society). Nicholas Bond, in the article
referred to, gives an example of a mother in desperate
need of a home. The 'radical casework' consisted of suggesting to her a number of measures she might try, ranging
from a visit to a councillor to a sit-in. The first
measure was successful. Such advice would seem to be
fairly common-sense. What the caseworker also did was to
build up the client's confidence in herself by praising
the measures she had already tried and encouraging her
determination and persistence in trying to get something
done. Such an attitude would also seem to be that which
one sensitive person might take to another in distress.
The caseworker also, obviously, sympathised with the
client's position, adopting it as his own on grounds,
presumably, of social justice.

Sunley ('Social Casework' June 1970) has listed fourteen
measures that a caseworker or an agency might use when
engaging in 'advocacy' on behalf of a client. They
include such measures as case conferences with other
agencies to enlist their help in a plan of campaign for
the client; position-taking: when the caseworker formally
takes up a position on the case through the media;
administrative redress through established government
machinery; petitions, etc. There are two measures he mentions with some hesitancy: demonstrations and protests
with the people concerned and with other professionals,

and the use of client groups - that is organising people
with similar life problems or problems with the same institution. In distinguishing these last two from the other
methods, Sunley is recognising something very important:
all advocacy methods place the client in a position dependent on the caseworker. The methods used by the case-
worker-advocate are of his own choosing. They are chosen
with reference to a professional norm. Involvement with
client groups places the caseworker in a situation in
which it is hard if not impossible to refer to professional standards: it is the client group which sets the standard now. This is collective action.

There is, however, nothing inherently radical or otherwise in any action or plan. Rein (1970) points out that:

> The purposes of social intervention theories, whether
> revolutionary or conservative, can either be directed
> at freeing men to build new standards or encouraging
> them to accept standards of prescribed behaviour. It
> is for this reason that an intervention strategy, sepa-
> rated from the purposes of intervention, does not
> provide the basis for a creed of radical [casework].

This should be obvious to us as we have shown that the
character of an action, or sequence of actions, depends in
part on the aims and intentions of the agent. Rein therefore quite correctly returns us to the ideology or beliefs
of the individual worker or the purposes informing a whole
plan of action or programme. He shows how a collective
action programme may not have the objective of bringing
about change but be simply designed to have a therapeutic
effect. This is because it has been found that involvement in action makes people feel better even if they do
not achieve their objectives. Thus in order to adjust
people to an unpleasant reality it may be worth engaging
them in an abortive campaign of action simply because they
will feel better and more accepting for having put up a
good fight !

The purposes that Rein suggests should inform either a
social worker, or a social-work programme, are moral ones.
He does not attempt to establish a model of a mentally
healthy, or ideal, society. He writes (1970):

> I believe that the great issue is social reform and
> that character ... is not the root of social problems.
> Redistribution, social justice, and participatory
> democracy are the crucial issues for change today.
> Social work must find its contribution to these ideals.
> It cannot rest content by working only with the insti-
> tutional fallouts of an inequitable system or by seek-
> ing to reduce public dependency by the use of social
> services.

Thus in asking the social caseworker to be concerned with social change he is not asking him to establish some ideal society or ideal pattern of personal relations, but simply asking him to work towards social justice - which we have already argued is entailed in a personal approach to casework. Further we have also seen that the caseworker is in no privileged position as a professional to decide moral issues such as what is social justice. Arguments of this sort he must (logically) participate in as a person. This does not deny that he may be in possession of relevant specialist knowledge. It is the relevance of this knowledge to issues of justice that can only be established as between persons. So, in having social justice as an objective, social casework is committed to the other two things mentioned by Rein. Participatory democracy is involved because issues of social justice and the differential treatment of people can only be fairly decided if those participating in the discussion and decision do so as equals. This goes a long way to ensuring that the decision is unforced and the product of the best arguments. Redistribution also entails social justice because it involves decisions as to how resources should be fairly (if differentially) allocated.

It should now be clear that what is described as 'radical casework' is consonant with the arguments put forward in establishing a personal approach to social casework. 'Radical casework' involves a socially critical stance based on the concept of social justice. It also involves an endeavour to change society or particular social institutions in so far as they are damaging to certain citizens. Attlee (1920) also adopted a similar position to this, but to it he added an objective for 'the social service movement' of building a society in which 'the good life' would be open to all.

The examples given by Rein, Bond and Sunley thus illustrate ways of working that can be adopted in a personal approach, and Sunley offers a list of methods that could similarly be used. What the personal approach can add to the current discussion and practice of radical casework is an understanding of some features that would have necessarily to appear in a society in which 'the good life' would be available to all. These features are derived from Milne's rational standard of critical humanism.

There remain, however, lacunae in the theory of radical casework. They are, I think, filled in a personal approach. People may, through no fault of their own, find themselves in emotional distress, more or less acute, and want help. What radical casework has to offer to such people is incomplete. Bond's first example indicates what damage may be done by using conventional methods of help that fail to take into account a person's life experience and prospects. His second example shows how an ordinary sympathy and direct advice as to how the client might deal with the practicalities of her situation brought emotional relief. It was not only because they were successful but also because they involved the client in doing something for herself, that these practical measures brought emotional relief. What Bond seems to be suggesting is that emotional and practical help can be offered at the same time by supporting the client in measures taken to remedy her social situation. The inference of this is that social and economic factors (rather than psychological) were at the root of her emotional condition. This may well be so, but there are other situations in which the relation between social situation and emotional problems is not so direct. Because it does not take account of these there are several criticisms that can be made of this position. First, it offers no solution to the client in whom emotional problems have, so to speak, taken root and which remain long after the social cause has been removed. Second, not all practical problems can be solved as readily as in the example offered by Bond. On occasion the methods he proposes might be used, as Rein suggests, quite cynically in order to achieve her adjustment to the practical situation: after putting up a good fight the mother might feel better and so accept the injustice of her situation. Third, it offers no solution to problems that are largely or entirely emotional and interpersonal in character. Fourth, by emphasising the importance of the client working on her own problem, the situation is ignored in which, because of deprivation and powerlessness, the client is unable to work on her problem whereas the social worker has the knowledge, status and power to do so.

Points two and four can be met from what has already been said in this section. Collective action, in which clients of similar experience and/or social position work together at a problem with methods chosen by themselves, can overcome the dependence on the social worker which opens up the possibility mentioned in item two. Collective action can also overcome the powerlessness of the individual client - as the trade union movement long ago discovered. Collective action does not, as we have seen, preclude the social worker joining in. Responsive to issues of social justice and aware of the deficiencies of society as one fit for persons, he can work as one of the collective.

Items one and three are difficult to accommodate within the radical-social-work model, because they do not involve an aspect of the problem in which co-operative (social worker and client) or collective action can be used as a way of solving the emotional within the practical problem. Is there a way of working on such problems that can in any way be called radical? I believe that the personal approach provides an answer.

It does so through its focus on personal identity. This demands that a person work on his own problems which Bond suggests is a criterion of radical social work. The requirements of an adequate and accurate description provide a method for the client to which the social worker is a guide. This, then, is the first responsibility of the social worker in a personal approach. In order that description and other activities may take place, the social worker's second responsibility is to encourage the development between himself and the client (group), and/or within the family or group, of relationships conducive to the growth and enrichment of personal identity. We have seen that a personal approach inevitably leads the social worker into family or group situations. A major task therefore is to help the family members establish relationships with each other in which each member (including the client) can develop an identity as a person. The skill required here is similar to that of being a sympathetic chairman. It involves helping the group to decide what members want to work on and then helping the others to give to the one speaking the necessary positive response so that description can take place adequately. Hopefully people will learn to do this for each other with less and less help from the social worker. This method is radical, as compared with conventional social casework, in that the worker is not doing things to people but participating in the construction of a social situation in which people can work on their own problems.

When an individual is working on his own emotional problem as in item one above, the personal planning of work on practical problems is usually replaced by continued description. There is a reciprocating movement between the past (as it becomes more accurately described) and the present for significance to be described and assessed. As this activity proceeds, a person's identity slowly changes. The past acquires a new significance in the present and so, too, do people from the past. For example many people have strong emotions to do with their parents, deriving from their experience as children. The parents may be dead, far away, or engaged with the client in a new adult relationship. The emotions from the past, however, still disturb the client and can be evoked powerfully in certain situations. In a personal approach the client will receive help from the social worker in working on such a problem himself. Beyond the task of description, the methods of co-counselling offer many possibilities. This particular method is relevant to a personal approach because it concentrates on teaching people to be clients and to work on their own problems (see Jackins, 1970). What the co-counselling movement prescribes for the person in the role of client are methods for acquiring self-knowledge - that is knowledge of oneself as a person. This we have seen Cavell describe as something that a person can learn. The co-counselling movement teaches people how this knowledge may be acquired.

It may be useful for the social worker to suggest sessions with relevant people from the client's past if their presence would help description; by and large, however, in describing the present significance of the past the client can work on his own with suggestions from the caseworker as to how he might proceed. He can, of course, work on his own without the presence of the social worker. Indeed, most people perform this task as part of ordinary life, though some do so less than others. It is only when there is a special difficulty that people will come to a social worker for help. In this situation, description of the past and of present significance of the past becomes formalised, so that the client (group) may learn how to do it.

As with practical problems, this way of tackling emotional problems is one that directly contributes to the client's identity as a person. In resolving the problem the client has learned methods of acquiring self-knowledge, the use of which enhances his identity as a person. He performs them in solving his problem and can use them whenever he likes in the future.

There may be situations in which the client is too distressed or hurt to overcome the problem in this way. In that case there are other methods, such as behaviour therapy, that can be tried. What I am suggesting here is that the social worker is the expert in helping people to learn how to cope with their emotional problems as persons, an expert in the methods of establishing and enhancing personal identity and helping others to acquire them.

In working on problems under item three of the criticisms of radical casework, the emotional problem lies in current relationships. The social worker's skill, here, lies in arranging and conducting meetings of people relevant to the resolution of the problem. Once more most of the work is description; description of what people are doing and feeling about each other now in the first

instance, and when this has been established, of their
significance to each other in the light of this.   People
in a family, for example, may begin to see each other in
new ways as a result of adequate and accurate description.
At the stage of proceedings we are now discussing, description will be focused on the new ways in which people
see each other.   This can be done verbally or by some of
the methods suggested by family therapists and the encounter movement.   For example one method is silent and
physical: one member of the family is asked to arrange the
others around him in terms of their closeness and attitude
to him.   One he may place behind another to indicate an
attempt to 'hide';   another he may place close to him with
fists raised to indicate hostility, etc.   The main task of
the social worker is to establish a situation in which
this can take place.   These are the conditions for the
establishment and enhancement of personal identity and
entail people making a positive contribution to each
other's attempts to describe actions, experience and new
significance.

Because this approach to emotional and interpersonal
problems is an educational one, the client learns how to
work on his own problems, and the social worker also
learns about the social conditions in which his clients
have lived their lives.   He sees how their attitudes and
values have been acquired from their cultural background
and how these are manifested in their relationships.
Esterson (1972) has shown how an analysis of this sort can
be made.   These sorts of considerations lead the social
worker to consider in what ways society could be, and
could have been, improved so that his clients could have
avoided calling on him for help.

The values and concepts on which relationships conducive to personal life depend are, as we have seen, honesty
and equality (of status) in descriptive agreement and the
choice of appropriate action; and a high standard of
rational thought and conduct culminating in critical
humanism.   To the extent that these are realised within a
family (or in personal action), then a culture supportive
of personal identity has been created.   It means that
family members will enable each other to be aware of the
character of their actions and experience;   it means that
there will be a thoughtful assessment of differential
treatment accorded to family members with the standards of
critical humanism being used;   it means that family members will try to find opportunities of self-realisation
for each other.   Many of these notions may be counter-
cultural (depending on the nature of the society or sub-
culture): that of rationality entails an allegiance to

social justice and a critical stance to society and its institutions; that of equality undermines the hierarchies of status in many social organisations and also in such institutions as the family where the various statuses of family members militate against that equality on which descriptive agreement and rational argument well nigh depend.

So a personal approach to social work with emotional and interrelational problems is radical in the sense that it entails allegiance to values, notions and activities that are critical and abrasive of society. Indeed criticism and change (in response to rational argument) are inherent in the way of life of the individual or society adopting the standards of critical humanism. To the extent, therefore, that the social worker succeeds in introducing, within families and groups, relationships conducive to personal growth, he succeeds in establishing ways of life that may be - and probably are, given the condition of current societies - in opposition to those prevailing in society at large.

So in its practical, its emotional and its interrelational aspects a personal approach to social work is as radical as and more comprehensive than radical social work. At the same time, however, we can see that it is no new departure. Aspects of it have been promulgated in the past by people like Attlee (1920), the traditional workers quoted in chapter 1, and conventional theorists such as Perlman. It has simply been a matter of bringing all together under the banner of personal identity.

I have talked throughout about a personal approach because it is not so much a matter of adopting new methods but of establishing current methods within a new framework. As Rein says, there is nothing inherently radical or conservative in any method. It is the purposes of those using them that breathe into them one or other of these characteristics. So the social-casework relationship has not been dispensed with but given a new character; self-determination continues to be important but in the new context of rationality; methods are still there but not for the social worker to use in changing the client's behaviour but for the client to use in developing his identity as a person in solving his problem. In addition the new 'radical' perspective is incorporated in the ways we have just seen. Under a personal approach a person is committed to a socially critical stance and has a concept of the sort of society that is conducive to personal life. Personal social work is therefore radical in its social perspectives. Its basis in rationality also involves it in encouraging the sort of measures to deal with practical problems advocated by Sunley, Bond and Rein.

We have seen the importance of Paulo Friere's model of the social caseworker-client/client-social caseworker dyad, in which each learns something from the other. Where description is concerned we noted that the client might learn various technical details from the social caseworker and the descriptive method: the caseworker might learn facts of the client's life experience and social situation. We argued that within this model it is important for the caseworker to respond to the facts of the client's personal experience and social situation in accordance with the same standard of rationality that he encourages the client to use. Where the consideration of methods is concerned it may well be that the client (or client group if the caseworker is involved in collective action) may want to engage in methods inimical or even abhorrent to the caseworker. Hilary Rose (1973) has described the difference of approach between semi-professional advocates and Claimants' Union representatives at Supplementary Benefit Tribunals. The methods of the semi-professional advocate are part of a social experience and culture shared with members of the tribunal. The methods of the Claimants' Union representative are part of the culture and social experience shared with the claimant. What the caseworker may have to learn is that the client may often be able to teach him the methods most likely to solve his problem. Certainly in collective action he is committed by his membership of the group to this possibility. This is, maybe, why Sunley quoted this as a measure of family advocacy with such hesitancy.

What happens in situations such as this is that people on each side of the discussion assess the appropriateness of alternative methods against different social experience. What seems reasonable and appropriate to the collective may not seem so to the caseworker. The only way in which the caseworker can share in this experience is if it is described to him. Oscar Lewis (1966) in his exploration of the lives of the deprived has shown what may be involved. Given that the caseworker is unable to enter into the clients' social experience and situation completely all he can do is accept the collective's judgment, provided that it takes account of questions of social justice, etc. Only if the fundamental values of honesty, promise-keeping and non-violence are threatened has he cause to withdraw from the collective's proposals.

This takes us back to the point made at the beginning of this chapter: that the standard for measuring the appropriateness of a course of action (both the ends and means) is its rationality. We can now see that while the

standards of rationality (as set forth by Milne for
instance) may be universally applicable, adherence to them
does not necessarily mean that a person can determine the
appropriateness or otherwise of a course of action. This
is because the appropriateness will, in part, depend on
the extent to which the action takes into account the
facts of the situation. This depends on an accurate description, especially of the facts of experience and action.
Further, under the Dominance Principle the agent's other
aims and objectives should be taken into account. So the
extent to which an action, or proposed action, is just
and/or rational from the standpoint of critical humanism
cannot be properly determined unless an accurate description of the situation it is designed to meet has been made.
This, as we have just seen and as Laing and Esterson
(1971) make clear, is a complex business. The point must
be emphasised that the social worker is in no position to
determine the rationality of an action because of all that
remains inaccessible to him about the client's situation.
All he can do is insist that people use criteria such as
Milne's in deciding what to do. He can, of course, be
more or less tactful and subtle in the way in which he
does this. So adopting Milne's standards of rationality
as the criteria of appropriateness of a course of action
does not mean that the social worker is in a position to
decide whether any particular action is appropriate or not.
All he is committed to is what any person as a person is
committed to: helping others to enhance their identity as
persons by acting rationally. In doing this he is enhancing his own identity as a person and fulfilling a moral
commitment to the principle of justice.

While personal social work helps people by means of
measures that contribute to their identity as persons, it
may well be that some people are unable to help themselves
in this way. At this point there is a skill to be
acquired in constructing social environments (therapeutic
communities) in which people may slowly learn to overcome
their emotional/psychological problems. At this stage the
approach being used is still personal and educational.
There may also, however, be people whose condition
requires some direct medical or other technically expert
help. Here we move into the area of chemo-therapy,
behaviour therapy, etc. It is not within the scope of
this volume to enter into the discussion as to what is
illness and what are 'problems of living'. What I am
suggesting is that there is a skill in developing one's
identity as a person, and this can be learned and taught.
Sometimes it may be simply the learning of this lesson
that will help a person. At other times the personal

method of solving problems may be learned as a problem is solved so giving the person increased mastery over himself and his environment in the future.

A personal approach to social work, with its focus on personal identity and action, therefore offers a way of thinking about and practising social work that encompasses the socially critical, even revolutionary, perspective of radical casework and a way of helping people with emotional and relationship problems that is radical in the sense of engendering values and ways of relating that are antipathetic, if not hostile, to a society falling short of the standards of critical humanism. This has not been noted by three social-work writers who have considered the question of personal identity. They have largely seen this in terms of role.

PERSONAL IDENTITY AND ROLE RELATIONS

Moffett (1968, pp.55-6) argues that the language of role does not fit well with casework method as expounded by Hollis (and Perlman). He argues that 'playing the parental role' is a method that involves all of Hollis's methods at once. Interest in role has certainly grown recently amongst casework theorists (e.g. Leonard, 1966; Perlman, 1966; Perlman, 1971; Ruddock, 1969). 'Role' is a technical term in the social sciences that has been developed to explain certain aspects of human activity - that is, what people actually do. 'Role' covers not only what people do but what people expect them to do. Perlman (1966, p.64) writes: 'Social roles mark out what a person in a given social position and situation is expected to be, to act like, and to feel like and what the other(s) in relation to him are expected to be, to act like and to feel like.' All that has been said above indicates how complex and how individual are the methods by which experience and action are characterised. If bus conductors are supposed to take fares certain general terms may be applicable to them in terms of sociological theory but what an individual conductor does and feels goes far beyond this, and varies from day to day according to the weather, his age, other events in his life, the different actions and feeling of those from whom he takes the fares, etc. All of this could be realised by describing it. How any particular bus conductor felt and acted on any occasion, if so rendered, could not be contained within the generalities of role concepts. The very terms of role theory entail that there is something about the person that extends beyond his role. For instance, people may

occupy more than one role and have in fact to manage them:
as teacher and father, a person may often have to manage
his roles in deciding when to go home, or how long to
spend mraking at night instead of playing with his children, etc. This implies that there is a person outside the
roles he occupies that manages the roles. This suggests
the existence of a person capable of experience beyond
what is offered in or expected of any one particular role.
We can also see that role explanations are designed to
explain what people are already doing. They are abstract
concepts derived from everyday life and re-applied to it.
People were acting and do act before role concepts can be
applied to them. What role may do is explain why and how
individuals as part of a whole society are brought together by forces within that society that they are not
aware of, but this does not describe their individual
experience or their actions in terms of the reasons and
objectives for their conduct. An exhaustive description
of the roles a person plays (his role 'tree' to use a term
of Ruddock's (1969, p.65)) does not render the person.
Personal identity goes beyond role-playing and is part of
a different sort of discourse from role which is technical
and sociological.

Perlman (1966, p.77) writes:

I suggest that problems of identity, at the time they
are seen by the caseworker (usually at a point of crisis
or of acute distress) are related to role problems. They
are related not only as they are explained by the person's previous and current role experiences. They are
also related as they may be ameliorated, if not resol-
ved, through a treatment focus upon helping the person
find, engage himself in, and derive rewards from some
vital role. Through such help his 'becoming' may be
signally affected.

She continued:

The essential point is that the carrying of one or more
vital roles at any stage of living is intimately
related to our sense of self, to our sense of who or
what we are.... We seek to establish identity not simply by being and belonging in certain social categories,
but by our being something and doing something in
relation to other people. Most of us best recognise
ourselves through what we do in our social interaction
in our relationships to people and to established life
tasks. I am myself, yes. But most of us are pushed
one step beyond - to define ourselves in social terms.
What we say to ourselves and to others ... is: 'I am a
wife....'

The task of the social caseworker becomes to help the
client 'to experience some valued role more satisfyingly'.
In 'carrying a social role a person does something and
therefore is something'. Perlman points out how empty and
valueless are the social roles that industrial society
makes available for some people. The caseworker aims to
help the individual interact in his own role more satis-
factorily by 'correcting' his perception of it, or by
helping him to find a role which he gets satisfaction from
carrying.

While Perlman criticises society for the roles it makes
available, the help that she describes the caseworker as
offering accepts the situation as it is. The caseworker
tries to alter the client's perception of his role or
assist him to find a new and more satisfying one. This is
all helpful but limited. Where personal identity is concerned Perlman recognises that what 'I do I am', but what
she sees a person as doing is carrying a role and getting
his satisfaction and identity through that. A person
becomes the role he carries. We have seen above that a
person is in fact separated from his roles and the theme
of all that has gone before is that a person's identity is
bound up with his biography as an agent in or out of a
role. A person is identified with all the separate acts
that he has performed. This is why description is of such
vital importance. This is why so much emphasis has been
given to rationality for the more considered a man's
actions the more certain will be his identity as an agent.
With actions at the habitual level he becomes what he does
willy-nilly. He has very little control over what he
does. At the level of social morality his identity is
limited to the actions that his society enables him to
perform. At the level of enlightened humanity he can act
in acoordance with criteria that relate to personal life
as such. He can in all his actions aim to make his own
and the personal life of others more adequate because he
knows what conditions have to be fulfilled to achieve this.
He does not have to accept the conventional mores and
values of his society when he acts. He is thus much more
in command of his own identity. It is from this point of
view that it is possible to consider the satisfactoriness
or otherwise of the roles one has to perform and the way
one is performing them.

AGENCY FUNCTION IN SOCIAL WORK

Most casework theorists conceive of the social-work agency
as the neutral setting for the practice of social casework.

Scant attention has been paid to its function in society
or its effect on social-casework practice (see Hollis,
1964; Perlman, 1957; Biestek, 1961). Smalley (1967),
however, argues that the major objective of social-work
practice is to forward the objectives of the agency. She
would probably agree with Timms (1964) that the aims and
values of a welfare agency are hardly likely to contravene
certain general humanitarian values.

Rein (1970) refers to the function of organisations and
institutions in creating problems for the social worker.
The organisation he refers to is school, but there are
many others - Social Security offices, housing departments,
public utilities, etc. Even social-service departments
create problems for clients who may then take them to
voluntary social-work agencies. So social workers in
various agencies may in fact create problems for each
other !

Jordan (1974, ch.7) has recently analysed the function
of social-service departments. He shows how they have
accepted functions not originally intended for them, e.g.
income maintenance in emergency situations, and how this
has affected social-work practice. His argument is that
specialist services originally intended for all citizens
(e.g. child care, mental health, medical after-care,
services for the elderly, etc.) now increasingly appear as
services, not for all citizens, but only for the poor and
deprived. So it becomes increasingly difficult for the
ordinary citizen to use such services without acquiring
the stigma of being a failure (for to use such services is
to suggest that one is poor, and to be poor in our com-
petitive society is somehow to have failed in the competi-
tion).

While we can accept at least the tenor of Jordan's
analysis of a social-work agency and applaud it as an
example of how all social workers should approach the
appraisal of their working situation, it is more difficult
to accept his analysis of social casework. The definition
with which he works is a limited one defining personal
care in terms of face-to-face contact and interview as
opposed to correspondence and administrative measures. He
also describes it (1974, p.104) as the expression of care,
love and compassion (see Halmos, 1965, 1970). Such
activity he sees as valuable in itself, which indeed it
is, but as we have seen above social caseworkers have
attempted far more than this in the giving of emotional
and psychological help. Jordan condemns the radical
critics of casework, saying that they should turn their
attention to the agencies whose change of function is
undermining the quality of social-work intervention rather

than attacking casework itself. He argues that, against
the background of the changes described in the last paragraph, social work is increasingly acquiring a controlling
function over the poor. This is because it offers emotional and psychological help to those whose needs are
primarily material and financial and whose problems Jordan
sees as deriving from the social structure rather than
individual pathology.

Jordan's limited view of social casework prevents him
from seeing the radical, or socially critical, element
latent in the traditional concern for the person. I hope
that the previous chapters have brought this hidden
element to the fore. If it had been developed earlier in
the history of the profession social workers might not
have been so naïve where changes in the function of their
agency were concerned.

Jordan (1974, p.107) also maintains that social casework can be practised 'virtually unrelated to the economic
demands of the productive system provided that certain
conditions are realised'. These conditions include the
functions of the employing agency. These should certainly
avoid income maintenance (and perhaps certain statutory
functions). (Another set of conditions involves emotional
and psychological support for the caseworker in his
arduous task.) This is in contradiction with much that has
been said previously. If social casework's main focus is
on personal identity then ethical and political issues are
bound to arise, often concerning the nature of society and
the economic system. And if, with Rein, we see clients'
problems being generated by the organisations and institutions of society then both caseworker and client should be
concerned about them and the economic and political
interests they serve.

In a society committed to the standards of critical
humanism, social workers and the agencies for which they
work should have the task of relating the views of the
unfortunate, the deprived and the underprivileged to
government as well as delivering a service. Indeed they
should have the task of forcing these views on government
when they are neglected. In a society not committed to
these standards the social worker, both as a citizen, and
also as one professionally committed to the standards of
critical humanism, has the task of trying to establish
these standards in individuals and groups. Agencies have
considerable changes to make if they are to facilitate a
personal social work committed to personal development,
with the fostering of counter-cultural values and socially
critical views and actions that this involves.

Bibliography

ANSCOMBE, G.E.M. (1963), 'Intention', Blackwell.
ARGYLE, M. (1969), 'Social Interaction', Methuen.
ATTLEE, C.R. (1920), 'The Social Worker', Bell.
AUSTIN, J.L. (1962), 'How To Do Things with Words', Oxford
University Press.
BATESON, G. et al. (1956), Toward a Theory of Schizo-
phrenia, 'Behavioural Science', I, 251-64.
BIESTEK, F.P. (1961), 'The Casework Relationship', Oxford
University Press.
BLANK, L. et al. (1971), 'Confrontation-Encounters in
Self-Awareness', Macmillan (New York).
BOND, N. (1971), The Case for Radical Casework, 'Social
Work Today', 29 July 1971.
BROOKE, R. (1972), Information and Advice Services, Bell.
CAVELL, S. (1958), Must We Mean What We Say?, 'Inquiry',
vol.I.
CAVELL, S. (1971), The Availability of Wittgenstein's
Later Philosophy, reprinted in Lyas, C. (ed.), 'Philosophy
and Linguistics', Macmillan; first appeared in 'Philo-
sophical Review', LXXI, 1962.
CHOMSKY, N. (1968, 1972), 'Language and Mind', Harcourt
Brace Jovanovich.
ESTERSON, A. (1972), 'Leaves of Spring', Penguin; first
published Tavistock, 1970.
FREIRE, P. (1972), 'Pedagogy of the Oppressed', Penguin.
FRIEDMAN, A.S. et al. (1965), 'Psychotherapy for the Whole
Family', Springer.
FREUD, A. (1937), 'Ego and Mechanisms of Defence', Hogarth.
HALEY, J. and HOFFMAN, L. (1968) (eds), 'Techniques of
Family Therapy', Basic Books.
HALMOS, P. (1965), 'Faith of the Counsellors', Allen &
Unwin.
HALMOS, P. (1970), 'The Personal Service Society', Allen &
Unwin.

HAMPSHIRE, S. (1958), 'Thought and Action', Chatto &
Windus.
HOLLIS, F. (1964), 'Casework - A Psycho-Social Therapy',
Random House.
JACKINS, H. (1965), 'The Human Side of Human Beings',
Rational Island Publishers.
JACKINS, H. (1970), 'Fundamentals of Co-Counselling
Manual', Rational Island Publishers.
JANOV, A. (1973), 'The Primal Scream', Abacus
JONES, M. and POLAK, O. (1968), Crisis and Confrontation,
'British Journal of Psychiatry', 114, 169-174.
JORDAN, W. (1974), 'Poor Parents', Routledge & Kegan Paul.
KENNY, A. (1963), 'Action, Emotion and Will', Routledge &
Kegan Paul.
KENNY, A. (1971), in Jones, O.R. (ed.), 'The Private
Language Argument', Macmillan.
LAING, R.D. (1967), 'Politics of Experience and The Bird
of Paradise', Penguin (1970).
LAING, R.D. (1969), 'Politics of the Family', CBC Publi-
cations.
LAING, R.D. (1970), 'Knots', Penguin.
LAING, R.D. and ESTERSON, A. (1971), 'Sanity, Madness and
the Family', Penguin; first published Tavistock, 1964.
LAING, R.D. et al. (1966), 'Interpersonal Perception',
Methuen.
LEONARD, P. (1966), 'Sociology in Social Work', Routledge
& Kegan Paul.
LEWIS, H.R. and STREITFELD, H.S. (1972), 'Growth Games',
Souvenir Press.
LEWIS, O. (1966), 'La Vida', Panther edition.
McDERMOTT, F.E. (ed.) (1975), 'Self-Determination in
Social Work', Routledge & Kegan Paul.
McINTYRE, A. (1967), 'Short History of Ethics', Routledge
& Kegan Paul.
McMURRAY, J. (1961), 'Persons in Relation', Macmillan.
MAYER, J. and TIMMS, N. (1970), 'The Client Speaks',
Routledge & Kegan Paul.
MELDEN, A.I. (1961), 'Free Action', Routledge & Kegan Paul.
MILNE, A.J.M. (1968), 'Freedom and Rights', Allen & Unwin.
MOFFETT, J. (1968), 'Concepts of Casework Treatment',
Routledge & Kegan Paul.
PERLMAN, H.H. (1957), 'Social Casework', Chicago Univer-
sity Press.
PERLMAN, H.H. (1966), The Social in Social Casework,
reprinted in Younghusband, E. (ed.), 'New Developments in
Casework', Allen & Unwin; first appeared in 'Social
Service Review', vol.XXXV, no.4, December 1961.
PERLMAN, H.H. (1971), 'Personna', Chicago U.P.

PETERS, R.S. (1958), 'The Concept of Motivation', Routledge & Kegan Paul.
PLANT, R. (1970), 'Social and Moral Theory in Social Case-work', Routledge & Kegan Paul.
REIN, M. (1970), Social Work in Search of a Radical Pro-fession, 'Social Work' (USA), October.
RICHARDS, D.A. (1971), 'A Theory of Reasons for Action', Oxford University Press.
ROBERTS, R.W. and NEE, R.H. (eds) (1970), Theories of Social Casework, University of Chicago Press.
ROSE, H. (1973), Who can de-label the claimant, 'Social Work Today', vol.4, no.13, 20 September 1973.
RUDDOCK, R. (1969), 'Roles and Relations', Routledge & Kegan Paul.
RYAN, A. (1970), 'The Philosophy of the Social Sciences', Macmillan.
SAINSBURY, P. (1970), 'Diagnosis in Social Casework', Routledge & Kegan Paul.
SINFIELD, A. (1969), 'Which Way for Social Work', Fabian Society.
SMALLEY, R.E. (1967), 'Theory for Social Work Practice', Columbia University Press.
SPIEGEL, J.P. (1960), The Resolution of Role Conflict in the Family, in Bell and Vogel (eds), 'The Family', Free Press.
STRAWSON, P.F. (1959), 'Individuals', Methuen.
SZASZ, T. (1962), 'Myth of Mental Illness', Paladin editions.
TIMMS, N. (1964), 'Social Casework', Routledge & Kegan Paul.
TIMMS, N. (1968), 'The Language of Social Casework', Routledge & Kegan Paul.
VENDLER, Z. (1967), 'Linguistics in Philosophy', Cornell University Press.
WILLIAMS, R. (1965), 'The Long Revolution', Penguin; first published Chatto & Windus,1961.
WINCH, P. (1958), 'The Idea of a Social Science', Routledge & Kegan Paul.
WITTGENSTEIN, L. (1968), 'Philosophical Investigations', Blackwell.

Index

Routledge Social Science Series

Routledge & Kegan Paul   London, Henley and Boston

39 Store Street, London WC1E 7DD
Broadway House, Newtown Road, Henley-on-Thames,
Oxon RG9 1EN
9 Park Street, Boston, Mass. 02108

Contents

*Authors wishing to submit manuscripts for any series in
this catalogue should send them to the Social Science Editor,
Routledge & Kegan Paul Ltd, 39 Store Street,
London WC1E 7DD*

● *Books so marked are available in paperback
All books are in Metric Demy 8vo format (216 × 138mm approx.)*

International Library of Sociology

General Editor   John Rex

GENERAL SOCIOLOGY

Barnsley, J. H. The Social Reality of Ethics. *464 pp.*
Belshaw, Cyril. The Conditions of Social Performance. *An Exploratory Theory. 144 pp.*
Brown, Robert. Explanation in Social Science. *208 pp.*
● Rules and Laws in Sociology. *192 pp.*
Bruford, W. H. Chekhov and His Russia. *A Sociological Study. 244 pp.*
Cain, Maureen E. Society and the Policeman's Role. *326 pp.*
●**Fletcher, Colin.** Beneath the Surface. *An Account of Three Styles of Sociological Research. 221 pp.*
Gibson, Quentin. The Logic of Social Enquiry. *240 pp.*
Glucksmann, M. Structuralist Analysis in Contemporary Social Thought. *212 pp.*
Gurvitch, Georges. Sociology of Law. *Preface by Roscoe Pound. 264 pp.*
Hodge, H. A. Wilhelm Dilthey. *An Introduction. 184 pp.*
Homans, George C. Sentiments and Activities. *336 pp.*
Johnson, Harry M. Sociology: *a Systematic Introduction. Foreword by Robert K. Merton. 710 pp.*
●**Keat, Russell,** and **Urry, John.** Social Theory as Science. *278 pp.*
Mannheim, Karl. Essays on Sociology and Social Psychology. *Edited by Paul Kecskemeti. With Editorial Note by Adolph Lowe. 344 pp.*
   Systematic Sociology: *An Introduction to the Study of Society. Edited by J. S. Erös and Professor W. A. C. Stewart. 220 pp.*
Martindale, Don. The Nature and Types of Sociological Theory. *292 pp.*
●**Maus, Heinz.** A Short History of Sociology. *234 pp.*
Mey, Harald. Field-Theory. *A Study of its Application in the Social Sciences. 352 pp.*
Myrdal, Gunnar. Value in Social Theory: *A Collection of Essays on Methodology. Edited by Paul Streeten. 332 pp.*
Ogburn, William F., and **Nimkoff, Meyer F.** A Handbook of Sociology. *Preface by Karl Mannheim. 656 pp. 46 figures. 35 tables.*
Parsons, Talcott, and **Smelser, Neil J.** Economy and Society: *A Study in the Integration of Economic and Social Theory. 362 pp.*
Podgórecki, Adam. Practical Social Sciences. *About 200 pp.*
●**Rex, John.** Key Problems of Sociological Theory. *220 pp.*
   Sociology and the Demystification of the Modern World. *282 pp.*
●**Rex, John** (Ed.) Approaches to Sociology. *Contributions by Peter Abell, Frank Bechhofer, Basil Bernstein, Ronald Fletcher, David Frisby, Miriam Glucksmann, Peter Lassman, Herminio Martins, John Rex, Roland Robertson, John Westergaard and Jock Young. 302 pp.*
Rigby, A. Alternative Realities. *352 pp.*
Roche, M. Phenomenology, Language and the Social Sciences. *374 pp.*

3

Sahay, A. Sociological Analysis. *220 pp.*
Simirenko, Alex (Ed.) Soviet Sociology. *Historical Antecedents and Current Appraisals. Introduction by Alex Simirenko. 376 pp.*
Strasser, Hermann. The Normative Structure of Sociology. *Conservative and Emancipatory Themes in Social Thought. About 340 pp.*
Urry, John. Reference Groups and the Theory of Revolution. *244 pp.*
Weinberg, E. Development of Sociology in the Soviet Union. *173 pp.*

FOREIGN CLASSICS OF SOCIOLOGY

● **Durkheim, Emile.** Suicide. *A Study in Sociology. Edited and with an Introduction by George Simpson. 404 pp.*
● **Gerth, H. H.,** and **Mills, C. Wright.** From Max Weber: *Essays in Sociology. 502 pp.*
● **Tönnies, Ferdinand.** Community and Association. *(Gemeinschaft und Gesellschaft.) Translated and Supplemented by Charles P. Loomis. Foreword by Pitirim A. Sorokin. 334 pp.*

SOCIAL STRUCTURE

Andreski, Stanislav. Military Organization and Society. *Foreword by Professor A. R. Radcliffe-Brown. 226 pp. 1 folder.*
Carlton, Eric. Ideology and Social Order. *Preface by Professor Philip Abrahams. About 320 pp.*
Coontz, Sydney H. Population Theories and the Economic Interpretation. *202 pp.*
Coser, Lewis. The Functions of Social Conflict. *204 pp.*
Dickie-Clark, H. F. Marginal Situation: *A Sociological Study of a Coloured Group. 240 pp. 11 tables.*
Glaser, Barney, and **Strauss, Anselm L.** Status Passage. *A Formal Theory. 208 pp.*
Glass, D. V. (Ed.) Social Mobility in Britain. *Contributions by J. Berent, T. Bottomore, R. C. Chambers, J. Floud, D. V. Glass, J. R. Hall, H. T. Himmelweit, R. K. Kelsall, F. M. Martin, C. A. Moser, R. Mukherjee, and W. Ziegel. 420 pp.*
Johnstone, Frederick A. Class, Race and Gold. *A Study of Class Relations and Racial Discrimination in South Africa. 312 pp.*
Jones, Garth N. Planned Organizational Change: *An Exploratory Study Using an Empirical Approach. 268 pp.*
Kelsall, R. K. Higher Civil Servants in Britain: *From 1870 to the Present Day. 268 pp. 31 tables.*
König, René. The Community. *232 pp. Illustrated.*
● **Lawton, Denis.** Social Class, Language and Education. *192 pp.*
McLeish, John. The Theory of Social Change: *Four Views Considered. 128 pp.*
Marsh, David C. The Changing Social Structure of England and Wales, 1871-1961. *288 pp.*
Menzies, Ken. Talcott Parsons and the Social Image of Man. *About 208 pp.*

●**Mouzelis, Nicos.** Organization and Bureaucracy. *An Analysis of Modern Theories. 240 pp.*

Mulkay, M. J. Functionalism, Exchange and Theoretical Strategy. *272 pp.*

Ossowski, Stanislaw. Class Structure in the Social Consciousness. *210 pp.*

●**Podgórecki, Adam.** Law and Society. *302 pp.*

Renner, Karl. Institutions of Private Law and Their Social Functions. *Edited, with an Introduction and Notes, by O. Kahn-Freud. Translated by Agnes Schwarzschild. 316 pp.*

SOCIOLOGY AND POLITICS

Acton, T. A. Gypsy Politics and Social Change. *316 pp.*

Clegg, Stuart. Power, Rule and Domination. *A Critical and Empirical Understanding of Power in Sociological Theory and Organisational Life. About 300 pp.*

Hechter, Michael. Internal Colonialism. *The Celtic Fringe in British National Development, 1536–1966. 361 pp.*

Hertz, Frederick. Nationality in History and Politics: *A Psychology and Sociology of National Sentiment and Nationalism. 432 pp.*

Kornhauser, William. The Politics of Mass Society. *272 pp. 20 tables.*

●**Kroes, R.** Soldiers and Students. *A Study of Right- and Left-wing Students. 174 pp.*

Laidler, Harry W. History of Socialism. *Social-Economic Movements: An Historical and Comparative Survey of Socialism, Communism, Co-operation, Utopianism; and other Systems of Reform and Reconstruction. 992 pp.*

Lasswell, H. D. Analysis of Political Behaviour. *324 pp.*

Martin, David A. Pacifism: *an Historical and Sociological Study. 262 pp.*

Martin, Roderick. Sociology of Power. *About 272 pp.*

Myrdal, Gunnar. The Political Element in the Development of Economic Theory. *Translated from the German by Paul Streeten. 282 pp.*

Wilson, H. T. The American Ideology. *Science, Technology and Organization of Modes of Rationality. About 280 pp.*

Wootton, Graham. Workers, Unions and the State. *188 pp.*

CRIMINOLOGY

Ancel, Marc. Social Defence: *A Modern Approach to Criminal Problems. Foreword by Leon Radzinowicz. 240 pp.*

Cain, Maureen E. Society and the Policeman's Role. *326 pp.*

Cloward, Richard A., and **Ohlin, Lloyd E.** Delinquency and Opportunity: *A Theory of Delinquent Gangs. 248 pp.*

Downes, David M. The Delinquent Solution. *A Study in Subcultural Theory. 296 pp.*

Dunlop, A. B., and **McCabe, S.** Young Men in Detention Centres. *192 pp.*

Friedlander, Kate. The Psycho-Analytical Approach to Juvenile Delinquency: *Theory, Case Studies, Treatment. 320 pp.*

Glueck, Sheldon, and **Eleanor.** Family Environment and Delinquency. *With the statistical assistance of Rose W. Kneznek. 340 pp.*

Lopez-Rey, Manuel. Crime. *An Analytical Appraisal. 288 pp.*
Mannheim, Hermann. Comparative Criminology: *a Text Book. Two volumes. 442 pp. and 380 pp.*
Morris, Terence. The Criminal Area: *A Study in Social Ecology. Foreword by Hermann Mannheim. 232 pp. 25 tables. 4 maps.*
Rock, Paul. Making People Pay. *338 pp.*
● **Taylor, Ian, Walton, Paul,** and **Young, Jock.** The New Criminology. *For a Social Theory of Deviance. 325 pp.*
● **Taylor, Ian, Walton, Paul,** and **Young, Jock** (Eds). Critical Criminology. *268 pp.*

SOCIAL PSYCHOLOGY

Bagley, Christopher. The Social Psychology of the Epileptic Child. *320 pp.*
Barbu, Zevedei. Problems of Historical Psychology. *248 pp.*
Blackburn, Julian. Psychology and the Social Pattern. *184 pp.*
● **Brittan, Arthur.** Meanings and Situations. *224 pp.*
Carroll, J. Break-Out from the Crystal Palace. *200 pp.*
● **Fleming, C. M.** Adolescence: Its Social Psychology. *With an Introduction to recent findings from the fields of Anthropology, Physiology, Medicine, Psychometrics and Sociometry. 288 pp.*
● The Social Psychology of Education: *An Introduction and Guide to Its Study. 136 pp.*
● **Homans, George C.** The Human Group. *Foreword by Bernard DeVoto. Introduction by Robert K. Merton. 526 pp.*
● Social Behaviour: *its Elementary Forms. 416 pp.*
● **Klein, Josephine.** The Study of Groups. *226 pp. 31 figures. 5 tables.*
Linton, Ralph. The Cultural Background of Personality. *132 pp.*
● **Mayo, Elton.** The Social Problems of an Industrial Civilization. *With an appendix on the Political Problem. 180 pp.*
Ottaway, A. K. C. Learning Through Group Experience. *176 pp.*
Plummer, Ken. Sexual Stigma. *An Interactionist Account. 254 pp.*
● **Rose, Arnold M.** (Ed.) Human Behaviour and Social Processes: *an Interactionist Approach. Contributions by Arnold M. Rose, Ralph H. Turner, Anselm Strauss, Everett C. Hughes, E. Franklin Frazier, Howard S. Becker, et al. 696 pp.*
Smelser, Neil J. Theory of Collective Behaviour. *448 pp.*
Stephenson, Geoffrey M. The Development of Conscience. *128 pp.*
Young, Kimball. Handbook of Social Psychology. *658 pp. 16 figures. 10 tables.*

SOCIOLOGY OF THE FAMILY

Banks, J. A. Prosperity and Parenthood: *A Study of Family Planning among The Victorian Middle Classes. 262 pp.*
Bell, Colin R. Middle Class Families: *Social and Geographical Mobility. 224 pp.*

Burton, Lindy. Vulnerable Children. *272 pp.*

Gavron, Hannah. The Captive Wife: *Conflicts of Household Mothers. 190 pp.*

George, Victor, and **Wilding, Paul.** Motherless Families. *248 pp.*

Klein, Josephine. Samples from English Cultures.
  1. Three Preliminary Studies and Aspects of Adult Life in England. *447 pp.*
  2. Child-Rearing Practices and Index. *247 pp.*

Klein, Viola. The Feminine Character. *History of an Ideology. 244 pp.*

McWhinnie, Alexina M. Adopted Children. *How They Grow Up. 304 pp.*

● **Morgan, D. H. J.** Social Theory and the Family. *About 320 pp.*

● **Myrdal, Alva,** and **Klein, Viola.** Women's Two Roles: *Home and Work. 238 pp. 27 tables.*

Parsons, Talcott, and **Bales, Robert F.** Family: Socialization and Interaction Process. *In collaboration with James Olds, Morris Zelditch and Philip E. Slater. 456 pp. 50 figures and tables.*

SOCIAL SERVICES

Bastide, Roger. The Sociology of Mental Disorder. *Translated from the French by Jean McNeil. 260 pp.*

Carlebach, Julius. Caring For Children in Trouble. *266 pp.*

George, Victor. Foster Care. *Theory and Practice. 234 pp.*
  Social Security: *Beveridge and After. 258 pp.*

George, V., and **Wilding, P.** Motherless Families. *248 pp.*

● **Goetschius, George W.** Working with Community Groups. *256 pp.*

Goetschius, George W., and **Tash, Joan.** Working with Unattached Youth. *416 pp.*

Hall, M. P., and **Howes, I. V.** The Church in Social Work. *A Study of Moral Welfare Work undertaken by the Church of England. 320 pp.*

Heywood, Jean S. Children in Care: *the Development of the Service for the Deprived Child. 264 pp.*

Hoenig, J., and **Hamilton, Marian W.** The De-Segregation of the Mentally Ill. *284 pp.*

Jones, Kathleen. Mental Health and Social Policy, 1845-1959. *264 pp.*

King, Roy D., Raynes, Norma V., and **Tizard, Jack.** Patterns of Residential Care. *356 pp.*

Leigh, John. Young People and Leisure. *256 pp.*

● **Mays, John.** (Ed.) Penelope Hall's Social Services of England and Wales. *About 324 pp.*

Morris, Mary. Voluntary Work and the Welfare State. *300 pp.*

Nokes, P. L. The Professional Task in Welfare Practice. *152 pp.*

Timms, Noel. Psychiatric Social Work in Great Britain (1939-1962). *280 pp.*

● Social Casework: *Principles and Practice. 256 pp.*

Young, A. F. Social Services in British Industry. *272 pp.*

SOCIOLOGY OF EDUCATION

Banks, Olive. Parity and Prestige in English Secondary Education: a Study in Educational Sociology. *272 pp.*

Bentwich, Joseph. Education in Israel. *224 pp. 8 pp. plates.*

●**Blyth, W. A. L.** English Primary Education. *A Sociological Description.*
1. Schools. *232 pp.*
2. Background. *168 pp.*

Collier, K. G. The Social Purposes of Education: *Personal and Social Values in Education. 268 pp.*

Dale, R. R., and **Griffith, S.** Down Stream: *Failure in the Grammar School. 108 pp.*

Evans, K. M. Sociometry and Education. *158 pp.*

●**Ford, Julienne.** Social Class and the Comprehensive School. *192 pp.*

Foster, P. J. Education and Social Change in Ghana. *336 pp. 3 maps.*

Fraser, W. R. Education and Society in Modern France. *150 pp.*

Grace, Gerald R. Role Conflict and the Teacher. *150 pp.*

Hans, Nicholas. New Trends in Education in the Eighteenth Century. *278 pp. 19 tables.*

● Comparative Education: *A Study of Educational Factors and Traditions. 360 pp.*

●**Hargreaves, David.** Interpersonal Relations and Education. *432 pp.*

● Social Relations in a Secondary School. *240 pp.*

Holmes, Brian. Problems in Education. *A Comparative Approach. 336 pp.*

King, Ronald. Values and Involvement in a Grammar School. *164 pp.*

School Organization and Pupil Involvement. *A Study of Secondary Schools.*

●**Mannheim, Karl,** and **Stewart, W. A. C.** An Introduction to the Sociology of Education. *206 pp.*

Morris, Raymond N. The Sixth Form and College Entrance. *231 pp.*

●**Musgrove, F.** Youth and the Social Order. *176 pp.*

●**Ottaway, A. K. C.** Education and Society: An Introduction to the Sociology of Education. *With an Introduction by W. O. Lester Smith. 212 pp.*

Peers, Robert. Adult Education: *A Comparative Study. 398 pp.*

Pritchard, D. G. Education and the Handicapped: *1760 to 1960. 258 pp.*

Stratta, Erica. The Education of Borstal Boys. *A Study of their Educational Experiences prior to, and during, Borstal Training. 256 pp.*

Taylor, P. H., Reid, W. A., and **Holley, B. J.** The English Sixth Form. *A Case Study in Curriculum Research. 200 pp.*

SOCIOLOGY OF CULTURE

Eppel, E. M., and **M.** Adolescents and Morality: *A Study of some Moral Values and Dilemmas of Working Adolescents in the Context of a changing Climate of Opinion. Foreword by W. J. H. Sprott. 268 pp. 39 tables.*

●**Fromm, Erich.** The Fear of Freedom. *286 pp.*

● The Sane Society. *400 pp.*

Mannheim, Karl. Essays on the Sociology of Culture. *Edited by Ernst Mannheim in co-operation with Paul Kecskemeti. Editorial Note by Adolph Lowe. 280 pp.*

Weber, Alfred. Farewell to European History: *or The Conquest of Nihilism. Translated from the German by R. F. C. Hull. 224 pp.*

SOCIOLOGY OF RELIGION

Argyle, Michael and **Beit-Hallahmi, Benjamin.** The Social Psychology of Religion. *About 256 pp.*

Glasner, Peter E. The Sociology of Secularisation. *A Critique of a Concept. About 180 pp.*

Nelson, G. K. Spiritualism and Society. *313 pp.*

Stark, Werner. The Sociology of Religion. *A Study of Christendom.*
  Volume I. *Established Religion. 248 pp.*
  Volume II. *Sectarian Religion. 368 pp.*
  Volume III. *The Universal Church. 464 pp.*
  Volume IV. *Types of Religious Man. 352 pp.*
  Volume V. *Types of Religious Culture. 464 pp.*

Turner, B. S. Weber and Islam. *216 pp.*

Watt, W. Montgomery. Islam and the Integration of Society. *320 pp.*

SOCIOLOGY OF ART AND LITERATURE

Jarvie, Ian C. Towards a Sociology of the Cinema. *A Comparative Essay on the Structure and Functioning of a Major Entertainment Industry. 405 pp.*

Rust, Frances S. Dance in Society. *An Analysis of the Relationships between the Social Dance and Society in England from the Middle Ages to the Present Day. 256 pp. 8 pp. of plates.*

Schücking, L. L. The Sociology of Literary Taste. *112 pp.*

Wolff, Janet. Hermeneutic Philosophy and the Sociology of Art. *150 pp.*

SOCIOLOGY OF KNOWLEDGE

Diesing, P. Patterns of Discovery in the Social Sciences. *262 pp.*

●**Douglas, J. D.** (Ed.) Understanding Everyday Life. *370 pp.*

●**Hamilton, P.** Knowledge and Social Structure. *174 pp.*

Jarvie, I. C. Concepts and Society. *232 pp.*

Mannheim, Karl. Essays on the Sociology of Knowledge. *Edited by Paul Kecskemeti. Editorial Note by Adolph Lowe. 353 pp.*

Remmling, Gunter W. The Sociology of Karl Mannheim. *With a Bibliographical Guide to the Sociology of Knowledge, Ideological Analysis, and Social Planning. 255 pp.*

Remmling, Gunter W. (Ed.) Towards the Sociology of Knowledge. *Origin and Development of a Sociological Thought Style. 463 pp.*

Stark, Werner. The Sociology of Knowledge: *An Essay in Aid of a Deeper Understanding of the History of Ideas. 384 pp.*

URBAN SOCIOLOGY

Ashworth, William. The Genesis of Modern British Town Planning: *A Study in Economic and Social History of the Nineteenth and Twentieth Centuries. 288 pp.*

Cullingworth, J. B. Housing Needs and Planning Policy: *A Restatement of the Problems of Housing Need and 'Overspill' in England and Wales. 232 pp. 44 tables. 8 maps.*

Dickinson, Robert E. City and Region: *A Geographical Interpretation 608 pp. 125 figures.*

The West European City: *A Geographical Interpretation. 600 pp. 129 maps. 29 plates.*

● The City Region in Western Europe. *320 pp. Maps.*

Humphreys, Alexander J. New Dubliners: *Urbanization and the Irish Family. Foreword by George C. Homans. 304 pp.*

Jackson, Brian. Working Class Community: *Some General Notions raised by a Series of Studies in Northern England. 192 pp.*

Jennings, Hilda. Societies in the Making: *a Study of Development and Re-development within a County Borough. Foreword by D. A. Clark. 286 pp.*

●**Mann, P. H.** An Approach to Urban Sociology. *240 pp.*

Morris, R. N., and **Mogey, J.** The Sociology of Housing. *Studies at Berinsfield. 232 pp. 4 pp. plates.*

Rosser, C., and **Harris, C.** The Family and Social Change. *A Study of Family and Kinship in a South Wales Town. 352 pp. 8 maps.*

●**Stacey, Margaret, Batsone, Eric, Bell, Colin,** and **Thurcott, Anne.** Power, Persistence and Change. *A Second Study of Banbury. 196 pp.*

RURAL SOCIOLOGY

Haswell, M. R. The Economics of Development in Village India. *120 pp.*

Littlejohn, James. Westrigg: *the Sociology of a Cheviot Parish. 172 pp. 5 figures.*

Mayer, Adrian C. Peasants in the Pacific. *A Study of Fiji Indian Rural Society. 248 pp. 20 plates.*

Williams, W. M. The Sociology of an English Village: *Gosforth. 272 pp. 12 figures. 13 tables.*

SOCIOLOGY OF INDUSTRY AND DISTRIBUTION

Anderson, Nels. Work and Leisure. *280 pp.*

●**Blau, Peter M.**, and **Scott, W. Richard.** Formal Organizations: *a Comparative approach. Introduction and Additional Bibliography by J. H. Smith. 326 pp.*

Dunkerley, David. The Foreman. *Aspects of Task and Structure. 192 pp.*

Eldridge, J. E. T. Industrial Disputes. *Essays in the Sociology of Industrial Relations. 288 pp.*

Hetzler, Stanley. Applied Measures for Promoting Technological Growth. *352 pp.*

Technological Growth and Social Change. *Achieving Modernization. 269 pp.*

Hollowell, Peter G. The Lorry Driver. *272 pp.*

●**Oxaal, I., Barnett, T.,** and **Booth, D.** (Eds). Beyond the Sociology of Development. *Economy and Society in Latin America and Africa. 295 pp.*

Smelser, Neil J. Social Change in the Industrial Revolution: *An Application of Theory to the Lancashire Cotton Industry, 1770–1840. 468 pp. 12 figures. 14 tables.*

ANTHROPOLOGY

Ammar, Hamed. Growing up in an Egyptian Village: *Silwa, Province of Aswan. 336 pp.*

Brandel-Syrier, Mia. Reeftown Elite. *A Study of Social Mobility in a Modern African Community on the Reef. 376 pp.*

Dickie-Clark, H. F. The Marginal Situation. *A Sociological Study of a Coloured Group. 236 pp.*

Dube, S. C. Indian Village. *Foreword by Morris Edward Opler. 276 pp. 4 plates.*

India's Changing Villages: *Human Factors in Community Development. 260 pp. 8 plates. 1 map.*

Firth, Raymond. Malay Fishermen. *Their Peasant Economy. 420 pp. 17 pp. plates.*

Gulliver, P. H. Social Control in an African Society: a Study of the Arusha, Agricultural Masai of Northern Tanganyika. *320 pp. 8 plates. 10 figures.*

Family Herds. *288 pp.*

Ishwaran, K. Tradition and Economy in Village India: *An Interactionist Approach.*
Foreword by Conrad Arensburg. 176 pp.

Jarvie, Ian C. The Revolution in Anthropology. *268 pp.*

Little, Kenneth L. Mende of Sierra Leone. *308 pp. and folder.*

Negroes in Britain. *With a New Introduction and Contemporary Study by Leonard Bloom. 320 pp.*

Lowie, Robert H. Social Organization. *494 pp.*

Mayer, A. C. Peasants in the Pacific. *A Study of Fiji Indian Rural Society. 248 pp.*

Meer, Fatima. Race and Suicide in South Africa. *325 pp.*

11

Smith, Raymond T. The Negro Family in British Guiana: *Family Structure and Social Status in the Villages. With a Foreword by Meyer Fortes. 314 pp. 8 plates. 1 figure. 4 maps.*

Smooha, Sammy. Israel: Pluralism and Conflict. *About 320 pp.*

SOCIOLOGY AND PHILOSOPHY

Barnsley, John H. The Social Reality of Ethics. *A Comparative Analysis of Moral Codes. 448 pp.*

Diesing, Paul. Patterns of Discovery in the Social Sciences. *362 pp.*

● **Douglas, Jack D.** (Ed.) Understanding Everyday Life. *Toward the Reconstruction of Sociological Knowledge. Contributions by Alan F. Blum. Aaron W. Cicourel, Norman K. Denzin, Jack D. Douglas, John Heeren, Peter McHugh, Peter K. Manning, Melvin Power, Matthew Speier, Roy Turner, D. Lawrence Wieder, Thomas P. Wilson and Don H. Zimmerman. 370 pp.*

Gorman, Robert A. The Dual Vision. *Alfred Schutz and the Myth of Phenomenological Social Science. About 300 pp.*

Jarvie, Ian C. Concepts and Society. *216 pp.*

● **Pelz, Werner.** The Scope of Understanding in Sociology. *Towards a more radical reorientation in the social humanistic sciences. 283 pp.*

Roche, Maurice. Phenomenology, Language and the Social Sciences. *371 pp.*

Sahay, Arun. Sociological Analysis. *212 pp.*

Sklair, Leslie. The Sociology of Progress. *320 pp.*

Slater, P. Origin and Significance of the Frankfurt School. *A Marxist Perspective. About 192 pp.*

Smart, Barry. Sociology, Phenomenology and Marxian Analysis. *A Critical Discussion of the Theory and Practice of a Science of Society. 220 pp.*

International Library of Anthropology

General Editor   Adam Kuper

Ahmed, A. S. Millenium and Charisma Among Pathans. *A Critical Essay in Social Anthropology. 192 pp.*

Brown, Paula. The Chimbu. *A Study of Change in the New Guinea Highlands. 151 pp.*

Gudeman, Stephen. Relationships, Residence and the Individual. *A Rural Panamanian Community. 288 pp. 11 Plates, 5 Figures, 2 Maps, 10 Tables.*

Hamnett, Ian. Chieftainship and Legitimacy. *An Anthropological Study of Executive Law in Lesotho. 163 pp.*

Hanson, F. Allan. Meaning in Culture. *127 pp.*

Lloyd, P. C. Power and Independence. *Urban Africans' Perception of Social Inequality. 264 pp.*

Pettigrew, Joyce. Robber Noblemen. *A Study of the Political System of the Sikh Jats. 284 pp.*

Street, Brian V. The Savage in Literature. *Representations of 'Primitive' Society in English Fiction, 1858–1920. 207 pp.*

Van Den Berghe, Pierre L. Power and Privilege at an African University. *278 pp.*

International Library of Social Policy

General Editor   Kathleen Jones

Bayley, M. Mental Handicap and Community Care. *426 pp.*

Bottoms, A. E., and **McClean, J. D.** Defendants in the Criminal Process. *284 pp.*

Butler, J. R. Family Doctors and Public Policy. *208 pp.*

Davies, Martin. Prisoners of Society. *Attitudes and Aftercare. 204 pp.*

Gittus, Elizabeth. Flats, Families and the Under-Fives. *285 pp.*

Holman, Robert. Trading in Children. *A Study of Private Fostering. 355 pp.*

Jones, Howard, and **Cornes, Paul.** Open Prisons. *About 248 pp.*

Jones, Kathleen. History of the Mental Health Service. *428 pp.*

Jones, Kathleen, with **Brown, John, Cunningham, W. J., Roberts, Julian,** and **Williams, Peter.** Opening the Door. *A Study of New Policies for the Mentally Handicapped. 278 pp.*

Karn, Valerie. Retiring to the Seaside. *About 280 pp. 2 maps. Numerous tables.*

Thomas, J. E. The English Prison Officer since 1850: *A Study in Conflict. 258 pp.*

Walton, R. G. Women in Social Work. *303 pp.*

Woodward, J. To Do the Sick No Harm. *A Study of the British Voluntary Hospital System to 1875. 221 pp.*

International Library of Welfare and Philosophy

General Editors   Noel Timms and David Watson

● **Plant, Raymond.** Community and Ideology. *104 pp.*

● **McDermott, F. E.** (Ed.) Self-Determination in Social Work. *A Collection of Essays on Self-determination and Related Concepts by Philosophers and Social Work Theorists. Contributors: F. P. Biestek, S. Bernstein, A. Keith-Lucas, D. Sayer, H. H. Perelman, C. Whittington, R. F. Stalley, F. E. McDermott, I. Berlin, H. J. McCloskey, H. L. A. Hart, J. Wilson, A. I. Melden, S. I. Benn. 254 pp.*

Ragg, Nicholas M. People Not Cases. *A Philosophical Approach to Social Work. About 250 pp.*

● **Timms, Noel,** and **Watson, David** (Eds). Talking About Welfare. *Readings in Philosophy and Social Policy. Contributors: T. H. Marshall, R. B. Brandt, G. H. von Wright, K. Nielsen, M. Cranston, R. M. Titmuss, R. S. Downie, E. Telfer, D. Donnison, J. Benson, P. Leonard, A. Keith-Lucas, D. Walsh, I. T. Ramsey. 320 pp.*

Primary Socialization, Language and Education

General Editor   Basil Bernstein

Adlam, Diana S., *with the assistance of Geoffrey Turner and Lesley Lineker.* Code in Context. *About 272 pp.*

Bernstein, Basil. Class, Codes and Control. *3 volumes.*
   1. *Theoretical Studies Towards a Sociology of Language. 254 pp.*
   2. *Applied Studies Towards a Sociology of Language. 377 pp.*
● 3. *Towards a Theory of Educatiomal Transmission. 167 pp.*

Brandis, W., and **Bernstein, B.** Selection and Control. *176 pp.*

Brandis, Walter, and **Henderson, Dorothy.** Social Class, Language and Communication. *288 pp.*

Cook-Gumperz, Jenny. Social Control and Socialization. *A Study of Class Differences in the Language of Maternal Control. 290 pp.*

●**Gahagan, D. M.,** and **G. A.** Talk Reform. *Exploration in Language for Infant School Children. 160 pp.*

Hawkins, P. R. Social Class, the Nominal Group and Verbal Strategies. *About 220 pp.*

Robinson, W. P., and **Rackstraw, Susan D. A.** A Question of Answers. *2 volumes. 192 pp. and 180 pp.*

Turner, Geoffrey J., and **Mohan, Bernard A.** A Linguistic Description and Computer Programme for Children's Speech. *208 pp.*

Reports of the Institute of Community Studies

●**Cartwright, Ann.** Parents and Family Planning Services. *306 pp.*
   Patients and their Doctors. *A Study of General Practice. 304 pp.*

Dench, Geoff. Maltese in London. *A Case-study in the Erosion of Ethnic Consciousness. 302 pp.*

●**Jackson, Brian.** Streaming: *an Education System in Miniature. 168 pp.*

Jackson, Brian, and **Marsden, Dennis.** Education and the Working Class: *Some General Themes raised by a Study of 88 Working-class Children in a Northern Industrial City. 268 pp. 2 folders.*

Marris, Peter. The Experience of Higher Education. *232 pp. 27 tables.*
   Loss and Change. *192 pp.*

Marris, Peter, and **Rein, Martin.** Dilemmas of Social Reform. *Poverty and Community Action in the United States. 256 pp.*

Marris, Peter, and Somerset, Anthony. African Businessmen. *A Study of Entrepreneurship and Development in Kenya. 256 pp.*

Mills, Richard. Young Outsiders: *a Study in Alternative Communities. 216 pp.*

Runciman, W. G. Relative Deprivation and Social Justice. *A Study of Attitudes to Social Inequality in Twentieth-Century England. 352 pp.*

Willmott, Peter. Adolescent Boys in East London. *230 pp.*

Willmott, Peter, and Young, Michael. Family and Class in a London Suburb. *202 pp. 47 tables.*

Young, Michael. Innovation and Research in Education. *192 pp.*

●Young, Michael, and McGeeney, Patrick. Learning Begins at Home. *A Study of a Junior School and its Parents. 128 pp.*

Young, Michael, and Willmott, Peter. Family and Kinship in East London. *Foreword by Richard M. Titmuss. 252 pp. 39 tables.*

The Symmetrical Family. *410 pp.*

Reports of the Institute for Social Studies in Medical Care

Cartwright, Ann, Hockey, Lisbeth, and Anderson, John L. Life Before Death. *310 pp.*

Dunnell, Karen, and Cartwright, Ann. Medicine Takers, Prescribers and Hoarders. *190 pp.*

Medicine, Illness and Society

General Editor W. M. Williams

Robinson, David. The Process of Becoming Ill. *142 pp.*

Stacey, Margaret, *et al.* Hospitals, Children and Their Families. *The Report of a Pilot Study. 202 pp.*

Stimson, G. V., and Webb, B. Going to See the Doctor. *The Consultation Process in General Practice. 155 pp.*

Monographs in Social Theory

General Editor Arthur Brittan

●Barnes, B. Scientific Knowledge and Sociological Theory. *192 pp.*

Bauman, Zygmunt. Culture as Praxis. *204 pp.*

●Dixon, Keith. Sociological Theory. *Pretence and Possibility. 142 pp.*

Meltzer, B. N., Petras, J. W., and Reynolds, L. T. Symbolic Interactionism. *Genesis, Varieties and Criticisms. 144 pp.*

●Smith, Anthony D. The Concept of Social Change. *A Critique of the Functionalist Theory of Social Change. 208 pp.*

Routledge Social Science Journals

The British Journal of Sociology. *Editor – Angus Stewart; Associate Editor – Leslie Sklair. Vol. 1, No. 1 – March 1950 and Quarterly. Roy. 8vo. All back issues available. An international journal publishing original papers in the field of sociology and related areas.*

Community Work. *Edited by David Jones and Marjorie Mayo. 1973. Published annually.*

Economy and Society. *Vol. 1, No. 1. February 1972 and Quarterly. Metric Roy. 8vo. A journal for all social scientists covering sociology, philosophy, anthropology, economics and history. All back numbers available.*

Religion. Journal of Religion and Religions. *Chairman of Editorial Board, Ninian Smart. Vol. 1, No. 1, Spring 1971. A journal with an interdisciplinary approach to the study of the phenomena of religion. All back numbers available.*

Year Book of Social Policy in Britain, The. *Edited by Kathleen Jones. 1971. Published annually.*

Social and Psychological Aspects of Medical Practice

Editor   Trevor Silverstone

Lader, Malcolm. Psychophysiology of Mental Illness. *280 pp.*

● **Silverstone, Trevor,** and **Turner, Paul.** Drug Treatment in Psychiatry. *232 pp.*

Printed in Great Britain by Unwin Brothers Limited
The Gresham Press Old Woking Surrey
A member of the Staples Printing Group